VANASPATI INDUSTRY IN INDIA

VANASPATI INDUSTRY IN INDIA

M.M. MATHUR

CONCEPT PUBLISHING COMPANY
NEW DELHI

The Indian Council of Social Science Research gave the financial support towards the publication of this work. However, the responsibility for the contents of the book—facts, opinions, conclusions, etc.—is entirely that of the author and not of the ICSSR.

First Published 1981

Murli Manohar **Mathur** (*b*. 1930-)

Published by

Naurang Rai
Concept Publishing Company
H-13, Bali Nagar
NEW DELHI-110015 (India)

Printed by

Patel Enterprises
at Sunil Printers, Naraina
New Delhi-110028

Dedicated to

my father

who toiled throughout his life to make mine

Preface

THIS work was originally completed in 1971 as a doctoral dissertation. The delay in publishing it in the present form was because I wanted to make some additions and alterations on the basis of as much material as I could collect from various sources like reports of the manufacturing units, published reports of the Government of India and its various departments, etc. During the spell the Government of India has initiated two measures which have a far-reaching impact on the vanaspati industry. In fact, in my original thesis, I had suggested both these measures. These are : (i) Lifting of the statutory price control on vanaspati, and (ii) exempting the industry from such levies as sales tax, octroi duties which differ from state to state and which create problems for the manufacturers as well as consumers. I had even suggested that the government should at least try to lift the price controls as these were adversely affecting the growth of the industry. The government ultimately lifted the price controls from 1 January 1975. This has had a salutary effect. There is a continuous production of vanaspati in adequate quantities. During 1980-81 for instance, against the total demand of 7.17 lakh tonnes of vanaspati the production from April to September alone was 3.56 lakh tonnes and this despite various fluctuations, in the supply position and the cost of the vegetable oil used by the manufacturers of vanaspati in the country. There is still no reduction in the production of vanaspati because the manufacturer knows that he can sell the production at an economic cost. The other suggestion I had made in my original thesis about the exemption of this industry from sales tax and octroi duties has also taken a practical shape. I am glad that the Chief Ministers' Conference held in September, 1980, in Delhi has taken a decision to exempt the vanaspati industry from both these levies.

Several suggestions to help the consumer and also the industry have been made in this study on which only the Government can take a decision. But it can be said with confidence that if these suggestions are shown due consideration all concerned would greatly benefit.

I am more than duly grateful to the Indian Council of Social Science Research which has given financial assistance for publishing this book. The views and the conclusions reached in this book are solely mine and not of the ICSSR.

M.M. MATHUR

Acknowledgements

I AM thankful to the librarians of (i) the Directorate of Economics and Statistics, Krishi Bhavan, New Delhi, (ii) the Planning Commission, Yojana Bhavan, New Delhi, (iii) the Federation of Indian Chambers of Commerce, and (iv) the Indian Council of World Affairs, Sapru House, New Delhi, for permission to use their libraries. In fact, I wrote the entire thesis in Sapru House.

I am also thankful to Shri A. C. Chhatrapati and Mr. Raj Kapila of the Vanaspati Manufacturers Association of India for the signal help rendered by them by making available various reports of the Association and discussing with me the problems which the industry has faced from time to time.

I am thankful to my friends Sarvashri Prem Singh and Kashmiri Singh for their encouragement to brush up the thesis and make it ready for publication.

Sarvashri Jagdish Lal, Harish Chander Arora and Miss Raj Bala have typed the manuscript of this book. I am thankful to them.

I have special thanks for my wife Suresh and son Anupam who have borne the real brunt during the preparation of the manuscript. Anupam has also helped me in checking the manuscript.

Last but not least, I am thankful to Concept Publishing Company, New Delhi, who have greatly encouraged me by bringing out this work.

M.M. MATHUR

Acknowledgements

I AM thankful to the librarians of (i) the Directorate of Economics and Statistics, Krishi Bhavan, New Delhi, (ii) the Planning Commission, Yojana Bhavan, New Delhi, (iii) the Federation of Indian Chambers of Commerce, and (iv) the Indian Council of World Affairs, Sapru House, New Delhi, for permission to use their libraries. In fact, I wrote the entire thesis in Sapru House.

I am also thankful to Shri A. C. Chaturvedi and Mr. Raj Khanna of the Vanaspati Manufacturers' Association of India for the great help rendered by them in making available various aspects of the Association and discussing with me the problems which the industry has faced from time to time.

I am thankful to my friends Shri Satish Prem Singh and Harbhajan Singh for their encouragement to finish up the thesis and make it ready for publication.

Shri Ramesh Lal, Harish Kumar Arora and Miss Raj Bala have typed the manuscript of this book. I am grateful to them.

I have special thanks for my wife Suresh and son Anupam who have been a constant source during the preparation of the manuscript. Anupam has also helped me in checking the manuscript.

Last but not least, I am thankful to Concept Publishing Company, New Delhi, who have greatly encouraged me by bringing out this work.

M.M. MATHUR

Contents

Preface 7

Acknowledgements 9

List of Tables 12

1. Introduction 15

2. Story of Margarine 18

3. Location of Vanaspati Industry 27

4. Manufacture of Vanaspati 37

5. Vanaspati : Production and Consumption 56

6. Capital Management and Labour 75

7. Economics of the Industry 81

8. Vanaspati and Consumer 88

9. Colouring of Vanaspati 95

10. Government and the Industry 100

11. Problems and Conclusions 113

Index 154

List of Tables

2 : 1 Per capita consumption of margarine and margarine-like fats in some major countries of the world in 1956 *20*

3 : 1 Regional distribution of units of vanaspati and area under groundnut production and production of groundnut during 1968-69 *28*

3 : 2 Generation of electric power at major power projects in India and the recipient states *32*

3 : 3 Stoppages of work and loss of man-hours during 1967-68 in West Bengal *35*

4 : 1 Production of groundnut and sesame oils in India from 1939-40 to 1949-50 *38*

4 : 2 Year-wise yield of five major oilseeds in India during the Fourth Five Year Plan *41*

4 : 3 Targets of production and area under oilseeds on the eve of the Fifth Five Year Plan *42*

4 : 4 The various uses for which vegetable oils are required *43*

4 : 5 The pattern of use of different oils in the manufacture of vanaspati *45*

4 : 6 Production of groundnut and groundnut oil from 1950-51 to 1979-80 *46*

4 : 7 Production of sesame oil during Five Year Plans *47*

4 : 8 Capacity of cottonseed milling in different States *49*

4 : 9 Production of cottonseed oil in India during 1950-51 to 1973-74 *50*

4 : 10 Quantity of cottonseed oil used in manufacture of vanaspati *51*

4 : 11 The number of tin container used by vanaspati manufacturers during the period 1955-65 *54*

5 : 1 World production of margarine, lard and other prepared facts during 1962-71 *57*

5 : 2 Production of margarine, lard and other prepared fats in different Asian countries during the period 1962-71 *58*
5 : 3 Production of vanaspati and installed capacity during the years 1930-46 *59*
5 : 4 Consumption, production and installed capacity of vanaspati in India during the First Plan period *60*
5 : 5 Export of vanaspati during 1951-52 to 1955-56 *60*
5 : 6 Consumption, production and installed capacity of vanaspati during the Second Plan period *61*
5 : 7 Consumption, production and installed capacity of vanaspati during the Third Plan period *63*
5 : 8 Year-wise estimate of consumption of vanaspati for the years 1969-74 *64*
5 : 9 Production and installed capacity of vanaspati during the years 1968-73 *64*
5 : 10 Production of vanaspati during the years 1974-75, 1978-1979 *65*
5 : 11 Purposes of consumption of vanaspati during the years 1960 and 1979 *66*
5 : 12 Distribution of production units of vanaspati according to installed capacity *68*
5 : 13 Regional pattern of production of vanaspati in India : 1962-70 *69*
5 : 14 Regional pattern of consumption of vanaspati in India : 1962-1970 *70*
5 : 15 Zonal pattern of production of vanaspati for a ten year period, 1966-76 *71*
5 : 16 Zonal pattern of production and consumption of vanaspati for the Five-Year period, 1966-70 *72*
6 : 1 Total capital investment in vanaspati industry from 1953 to 1971 *75*
6 : 2 Working and fixed capital invested in vanaspati industry in India between 1953 and 1971 *76*
6 : 3 Percentage of different categories of workers required in vanaspati industry *78*
8 : 1 Sale of vanaspati in India during 1935-1946 *88*
8 : 2 Regional pattern of consumption of vanaspati for the period 1966-1976 *90*

8 : 3 Zonal distribution of percentage consumption of vanaspati *91*
11 : 1 Import of vegetable oil during 1965-75 *114*
11 : 2 Per-acre yield of groundnut and sesame in India and some other countries of the world *115*
11 : 3 State-wise irrigated area under groundnut *121*
11 : 4 Index number of wholesale prices of groundnut and sesame oil for 1952-53 to 1968-69 *133*
11 : 5 Wholesale price index of groundnut oil during 1973-74 to 1977-78 *134*
11 : 6 Prices of sesame, groundnut and vanaspati during April, 1976 to October, 1977 *135*
11 : 7 Highest and lowest prices of groundnut oil during 1962-1970 *137*
11 : 8 Requirements of electricity for vanaspati manufacture *141*
11 : 9 Foreign exchange earned by export of vanaspati during 1951-52 to 1965-66 *144*
11 : 10 Rates of excise duty on vanaspati, 1957-58 to 1975 *145*
11 : 11 Gross profits in vanaspati industry *148*
11 : 12 Gross profits as percentage of sales and capital of 10 companies with predominant interest in vanaspati industry, 1963 64 to 1969-70 *149*
11 : 13 Return on capital employed in vanaspati industry for the period 1966-1975 *150*

1

Introduction

VANASPATI industry is one of the most important food industries in India. It is next to sugar in so far as its essentiality in the daily life is concerned. It was first set up in the country during the British rule in spite of the fact that the British were opposed to any development of this country especially the industrial development. It is now 50 years old.

To present a clear picture of the industry the study has been divided into 10 chapters besides the introductory chapter. Chapter Two deals with the story of margarine, its early history of how and when it was invented. How it was introduced in India and where and when the first vanaspati manufacturing unit was set up. It also deals with the difficulties the industry faced during the initial period and with the development of industry in the subsequent years.

Chapter Three examines the theory of location of industries as is applicable to vanaspati industry in India. Various factors which have played important roles in the setting up of units of vanaspati industry in different parts of the country have been discussed.

Chapter Four deals with the raw materials required for the manufacture of vanaspati. Since the most important raw material required is vegetable oil, this chapter deals with the production of vegetable oilseeds, with the characteristics of various vegetable oils and their comparative utility in the manufacture of vanaspati. The production of oilseeds during different periods of time, since the vanaspati industry was set up in the country, has also been dealt with. The progress made in the production of various vegetable oils during the

Five Year Plans has also been reviewed. It also deals with the gradual change in the use of various vegetable oils in vanaspati manufacture during the course of its long life.

In Chapter Five, the production of vanaspati from the very first year of its production has been dealt with. It also deals with the various difficulties that the industry faced in the production of vanaspati during the long period of its growth in the country. It also deals with the comparative study of production of vanaspati in various Five Year Plans. It also examines the development of this industry in the various regions of the country and also attempts to find an answer to the question, why production in one zone is more than in the other.

Chapter Six deals with the capital, management and labour vis-a-vis vanaspati industry. It tries to find an answer to questions like, why this industry has never faced the problem of investment, why the industry has idle capacity. Various types of managements which are found in this industry have also been discussed.

Chapter Seven deals with the cost of production of vanaspati. Based on information from various sources like Tariff Commission reports and on personal discussions with the production managers of the industry, the cost of different stages of manufacture of one tonne of vanaspati has been calculated.

Vanaspati industry is a consumer industry. It is directly consumed, and as such the difficulties of the consumer matter much in this industry. Also having gained immense popularity among the consumers in the country, its consumption has steadily increased. All this has been shown in Chapter Eight with the help of facts and figures. In addition, the pattern of regional consumption of vanaspati has been shown.

The industry has faced a great controversy on the colouring of vanaspati from the very first day of its production. Why colouring is needed and how it can be done. Does it or does not need colouring are the questions discussed in Chapter Nine.

Chapter Ten deals with the Government policies towards this industry. Various controls on its production and on the maintenance of nutrition element of vanaspati have been discussed in this Chapter.

The last Chapter deals with the various problems faced by this industry. Some measures have been suggested for the possible solutions of these problems.

2

Story of Margarine

CHEMICAL Industry is regarded as one of the giants of the technological world. An offshoot of this industry is the synthetic industry. With the development of chemical industry it has become possible to produce a multitude of synthetic articles essential for daily use out of such raw materials as coal, salt, limestone, sulphur, air, petroleum and even water. Synthetic industry has successfully produced synthetic cloth, synthetic rubber, synthetic vitamins and synthetic fats as well.

Synthetic fat has revolutionized the food industry. The rich and nutritive qualities of this fat have made it an important item of daily diet of the rich and poor alike.

The necessity for producing synthetic fat or machine fat, as it is popularly known these days, arose because of an acute shortage of butter in Europe during the 19th century. It was known as Butterine[1] but later named as margarine in honour of the French chemist, Hippolyte Mege Mouries,[2] who invented it in 1869.

During the 19th century the economic condition of Europe was very bad and those belonging to the poor class could not afford butter. They lived mainly on potatos. Those who were slightly less unfortunate could afford little bread along with potatos and added a little tea to break the monotony of diet. Butter was beyond their purse. The workmen who earned better wages during those days could afford to use butter. By the end of the 19th century the working class whose number was still swelling were in the dire need of a cheap substitute for butter.

It was under these circumstances that Napolean III, the King of France, promoted a competition[3] among French chemists with the sole purpose of producing a cheap substitute for butter. He had two intentions. Firstly, the betterment of the working class and, secondly, economy in the supply of food to the French army. Mege solved the problem, although in principle only, by establishing that the liquid particles if passed through the kidneys of cows and subsequently through the udders could turn into milk containing butter. It was also established that by treating the fat in which the kidneys were enveloped and by adding udders in a sliced form a substitute for butter[4] could be obtained.

The method of obtaining it was that first the kidney fat was treated by melting it and cleaning the melted fat with rough salt. The salt sank to the bottom of the vat taking the dirt and fibre along with it. The purified fat was allowed to solidify to the point at which it became granulated. The resulting substance was called premier jus.[5] It was then pressed through a thin cloth. The oil discharged was called Olao.[6] In fact it was Olao which formed the basis of the butter substitute. In order to obtain the final product Olao was churned with milk and sliced udders. Mege was able to carry his research up to this stage only. The thread of further research in this direction was picked up by other chemists. This process offered big potential for research and was later developed on commercial lines.

For edible purposes and many commercial applications it was felt desirable to have solid fats. The great development of margarine and shortening products resulted from the invention of a successful method of converting low melting unsaturated fatty acids and glycerids in to much higher melted saturated products.

Hydrogenated vegetable oils in the present form were processed in the year 1910, with the introduction of the system known as catalytic hydrogenation.[7] The circumstances which prompted such an invention were the shortage and rising prices of animal fat. Introduced by America this process helps convert liquid oils into semi-liquids.

Introduction of the process of hydrogenation made shortening and margarine from vegetable oils as substitute for cooking fat and butter respectively very popular among the Western countries. Even now those countries which were traditionally known as butter/ghee-consuming countries have begun consuming the synthetic fats in quantities three or four times more than butter or ghee. In America the consumption of margarine rose almost three times in 1956 as compared to that in 1940. Butter consumption was nearly halved during a sixteen-year period (1940-56).[8] This phenomenon has been illustrated in Table 2.1 which shows per capita consumption of margarine, shortening and milk fats like butter and ghee in various countries of the world.[9]

TABLE 2.1

Per capita Consumption of Margarine and Margarine like fats in Some Major Countries of the World in 1956

Country	Margarine and Decreasing Consumption (kg. per year)	Consumption of Milk Fats like Butter & Ghee (kg. per year)
Denmark	28	9
West Germany	25	6
United Kingdom	24	8
U.S.A.	21	8
New Zealand	21	11
Canada	20	7
Australia	15	7
U.A.R.	7	3
India	4	3

Table 2.1 shows that countries like Denmark and Holland which are responsible respectively for 29 per cent and 5 per cent of the total world production of butter are consuming more than two to four times margarine than butter. Indians, however, still prefer butter to margarine because of the belief that margarine is prepared from animal fats which because of strong religious sentiments, does not suit most of them who are vegetarians.

Vanaspati

These synthetic fats are known in India by different names such as 'Vanaspati', 'Dalda ghee', 'Hydrogenated oil', etc. The term has been defined in the latest edition of Webster's dictionary as "a hydrogenated vegetable fat used as a butter substitute in India".[10] Perhaps because vanaspati ghee is manufactured with vegetable oils and there is not much change in the components of vegetable oils after it has undergone the process of refining and hydrogenation, the name 'vanaspati' has been given to this refined oil. The term has now been accepted and is popularly known as vanaspati ghee. On the basis of processing, vanaspati ghee has been defined "as the hydrogenated oil which has been subjected to a process by which hydrogen is added to the molecules of the oil to make it semi-solid instead of liquid".[11]

During the early thirties scarcity of ghee began to be felt in India because of various reasons like growth of population, conversion of pasture lands into agricultural lands resulting in reduction in cattle population, development of urban areas and demand for more milk from these areas, the rising standard of living of the people after the First World War, etc. The need for some cheap substitute to the traditional ghee for preparing their dishes was therefore keenly felt by the people.

Thus the story of vanaspati in India goes back to almost 50 years when it made its first appearance on the shelves of Indian shops through imports from Holland. With the appearance and flavour akin to those of the traditional ghee, its relative cheapness soon made it very popular among the Indian masses.

India then was the principal supplier of edible oils to the European countries which manufactured margarine. It was considered by the British rulers more economical to establish a vanaspati factory in India itself instead of exporting vegetable oils and oilseeds and then importing processed oils from the same countries. This is the reason why, when the whole world was enveloped by the thick clouds of great depression in the thirties, two vanaspati factories came into existence in India in 1930. The first factory was set up by the Indian Vegetable Product Ltd., Bombay, with an installed capacity of 303 tons of vanaspati per annum. It was soon followed by the Ganesh Flour Mill Co. Ltd, Lyallpur (now in Pakistan). They had a total installed capacity of 10,000 tons.[12] These were followed by the Tata Oil Mills Co. Ltd. and the Hindustan Vanaspati Manufacturing Co. Ltd. owned by the Hindustan Lever Ltd. at Ernakulam and Bombay respectively. U.P. had its first vanaspati factory in Kanpur in 1934, owned by the Ganesh Flour Mills Co., Ltd.

As production of vanaspati gradually increased and more and more factories were established the imports declined. Whereas in 1928-29, 22,909 tons of vanaspati were imported, in 1939-40 the total imports were only to the extent of 279 tons.

Indian vanaspati industry was fortunate in the beginning in that the Government of India looking for more revenues to meet its deficit budget imposed a heavy import duty on vanaspati. This enabled the industry to capture the market already established by the importers. So, three more factories were established in 1935.

The Second World War proved to be a boon for the vanaspati industry in India. The 'desi' ghee which was available at Rs. 0.75 paise per pound before the outbreak of the war was selling at Rs. 3 per pound during the war-period.[13] Growing urbanization and war-time economic conditions also gave a boost to the demand for vanaspati. Gradually it exceeded the total installed capacity of all vanaspati factories. There was shortage, and it was felt so intensely that the Government of India had to intervene. Thus, the first ever control on the price of vanaspati was imposed by the Government of India in 1943.

Vanaspati had become very popular immediately after it was introduced among the masses in India. Its sale rose from 18,000 tons in 1935 to 1,37,000 tons in 1946 i.e. by 761 per cent. By 1945 the number of factories had also increased to 21.

In 1939, Vanaspati Manufacturers' Association of India was formed. It was recognized in 1946, and was ultimately incorporated as a public company on 13 June, 1967.

It began to function as a company from 1st August, 1967. The main objects of the Association, as envisaged in the Memorandum of Association,[14] are:

(i) To promote and protect the trade, commerce and sale of vanaspati manufactured in India;

(ii) To promote and organize scientific research calculations to advance the trade and manufacturing of vanaspati and allied products.

It, in fact, acts as the spokesman of the industry.

In the immediate post-war period there was a rush to establish new vanaspati factories because there was "glow of gold"[15] about every vanaspati industry during the war. The Post-war Reconstruction Committee estimated that the demand for vanaspati would rise three times in five years. That is why the Committee encouraged, through licensing, establishment of 62 factories of varying sizes in all parts of the country. During 1946 alone, the number of factories was 22.

However, the years 1946-48 were bad years for the Indian vanaspati industry. In 1946 the industry had to face criticism from Mahatma Gandhi[16] who strongly opposed the growth of this industry because, according to him, it adversely affected the rural economy. This had a bad effect on the growth of this industry in India. During 1947, doubts about the nutritive value of vanaspati were aired by the consumers. This not only prejudiced a large number of consumers but even influenced the Government's decision on vanaspati prices, and control. The industry had to struggle even for its survival.

Fortunately for the industry, in 1950 vanaspati was declared to be a wholesome food fit for consumption as a fat. It was after receipt of this clearance that the attitude of the Government and makers of public opinion softened considerably. The control on the vanaspati was removed in 1952. The industry was included in the Schedule of the Industries (Development and Regulation) Act with the result that regular development of the industry was ensured.

At the beginning of the First Five Year Plan (1951) there were 49 vanaspati factories in production. Ten factories were under construction. This number rose to 58[17] at the end of the First Plan.

During the course of the Second Five Year Plan the number of units actually went down to 55 only.[18] This was because three factories which were producing vanaspati in the First Plan period suspended production during the Second Plan.

During the Third Plan also the number of factories went down. There were only 52 factories producing vanaspati in the country on 31 March, 1966.[19] However, the industry received a sudden fillip in 1968 when the Government of India decided, as a policy, to suspend the requirement of an industrial licence for establishing new units and or expanding the existing ones for all industries in the country.

Although the Government reimposed licencing for vanaspati units in February, 1970, mainly because of the apprehension of an inadequate supply of edible oils,[20] as many as 47 requests[21] were received from different parts of the country by the Directorate of Sugar and Vanaspati for setting up new factories as well as for enhancing production capacity of existing vanaspati industry. The licensed capacity of the industry rose to 17 lakh tons in 1974[22] from 7 lakh tons in 1969. This was due to the fact that licences to 28 factories with additional 3 lakh tons were issued to new entrants to vanaspati manufacture in 1971. In addition seven old manufacturers were given licences either for expansion of their existing plants or for setting up new plants in January, 1971.

Thus, in 1971, the total licensed capacity of vanaspati industry was 14 lakh tons per annum. The installed capacity was, however, 12 lakh tons per year, i.e. 2 lakh tons less than the licensed capacity. But the actual production of vanaspati never went beyond 6 lakh tons per year.

At present vanaspati production is in the neighbourhood of 6.50 lakh tons. It is sufficient to meet the demand of the country. The industry has a total installed capacity of about 13 lakh tons. This is sufficient to meet the demand of the people during the next decade. Thus investment-wise there are no requirements for vanaspati industry in the country.

The Vanaspati Manufacturers' Association of India announced on 6 May, 1977, a six-point plan which included maximization of production of vanaspati. It shows that though there is sufficient production/installed capacity of vanaspati in India the production is lagging behind and the steps announced by the VMA are in that direction alone.

The popularity this industry has gained during the last decade can be judged from the fact that vanaspati has become an important article of diet of every Indian whether rich or poor. Any change in its price or shortage in its supply attracts wide publicity in the Press and in Parliament. The Government as well as Opposition leaders pay immediate attention to its problems. If the industry is able to get continuous supply of edible oils required for its manufacture it is certain that the future of this industry is very bright. It would not only be giving employment to a very large number of persons in the country but can also become a rich foreign exchange earner by exporting to countries in the Middle East and even to the U.K.

And as already said, its being considered a nutritive fat measured by any yardstick, viz. digestibility, stability and even caloric value, has ensured a bright future for this industry in India.

REFERENCES

1. Charles Wilson, *The History of Unilever*, Cassel & Co., London, 1954, Vol. II, p. 26.
2. *Encyclopaedia Britannica*, Vol. 14, p. 854.
3. ibid, n. 1.
4. *Encyclopaedia Americana*, American Corporation, New York, 1958, Vol. 18, p. 279.
5. Wilson, n. 2, p. 25.
6. ibid.
7. *Industrial Development in Asia and Far East*, United Nations, New York, Vol. II, p. 296.
8. *Encyclopaedia Americana*, n. 4, p. 279.
9. *Eastern Economist* (Quarterly), New Delhi, August, 1965.
10. *Webster, Third New International Dictionary.*
11. C.S.I.R., *Investigation on the Consumption and Nutritive Value of Vanaspati*, CSIR, New Delhi.
12. G. D. Binani, and T. V. Ramarao, *India at a Glance*, Orient Longman's Ltd., Calcutta, 1954, p. 1161.
13. *Indian Year Book 1942-43*, Times of India Press, Bombay, p. 706.
14. Vanaspati Manufacturers Association, *Memorandum of Association.*
15. A. C. Chhatrapati, *Financial Express*, Bombay 7, 25 November, 1970, pp. 6-8.
16. ibid.
17. *Programme of Industrial Development 1956-61*, Planning Commission, New Delhi, pp. 416-17.

18. *Programme of Industrial Development, 1961-66*, Planning Commission, Planning Commission, New Delhi, pp. 676-7.
19. *Rajya Sabha Debates*, Part 2, Vol. 58, Nos. 18-25, Unstarred Question No. 696 on 5 December, 1966.
20. *Oil and Oilseed*, Oil and Oilseeds Association, Bombay, February, 1971, p. 8.
21. Personally verified from the Directorate of Sugar and Vanaspati, Government of India, New Delhi.
22. Estimates Committee Report of the 5th Lok Sabha 1974, *Economic Times*, 5 June, 1970.

3

Location of Vanaspati Industry

VANASPATI Industry is a raw material and consumption-oriented industry. Till recently groundnut oil was the main raw material for vanaspati. Groundnut is produced largely in central, western and southern India. It loses its weight only three to five per cent as waste which is called soap stock. Even the soap stock is used for the manufacture of washing soap. In Haryana, U.P., Punjab, Rajasthan and Delhi there are 10 units accounting for a total production of about 4 lakh tonnes of vanaspati.

These are the centres where production of groundnut oil, sesame oil or cottonseed oil is not enough and, therefore, vegetable oil used in these units is imported from the southern or western parts of the country. On the other hand in the States which are rich in this raw material, the concentration of vanaspati industry is not in the interior of the States but in the urban areas. Bombay, Mysore, and Madras cities, for example. The only explanation for such a concentration is that these cities are mostly vanaspati-consuming areas.

Similarly, if we examine the vanaspati industry from the other point of view, we find that it is concentrated at the centre where groundnut oil is produced in great quantity. It will be seen from Table 3.1 that out of the 51 vanaspati-producing units Maharashtra, Gujarat, Tamil Nadu and Mysore alone account for 25 which is nearly 50 per cent of the total units in the country. These four States account for a total of 63.68 per cent of the total area of the country under groundnut cultivation and produce 61.84 per cent of the total groundnut production in the country.

TABLE 3.1

Regional Distribution of Units of Vanaspati, and Area under Groundnut Production and Production of Groundnut during 1968-69[1]

State	No. of Units	Area under groundnut in (000) hectare	Production of groundnut in (000) tons
Maharashtra	10	1000.4	743.9
Gujarat	5	1798.0	806.2
Tamil Nadu	5	882.6	837.04
Mysore	5	801.5	380.7
Total	26	4482.5	2768.2
Total All-India	51	7091.2	4475.8
Percentage	49	63.63	61.84

These States primarily consume raw vegetable oil. Yet these have so many vanaspati-producing units. The vanaspati produced by these States is sold in the northern region and is transported there. This proves that vanaspati is a raw material industry also. The Census report has also supported the contention that vanaspati is a raw material-oriented industry. It has been stated that:

> In some districts industry is raw material-oriented. Thus the groundnut growing areas of Rayalaseema, North-Western Maharashtra and Gujarat State supply the necessary raw material to the hydrogenated oil mills in Kurnool, Jalgaon and Ahmedabad districts respectively. The large production of copra from coconut in Kerala support the Trichur hydrogenated oil factory in Kerala.[2]

Vanaspati is a market-oriented industry also. It is supported by the installation of new units in two years after the withdrawal of licensing restrictions in 1968. In the northern zone the number of units increased three times[3] between 1970 and 1971 than what these were on 31 January 1969. The reason is that in this zone there is the maximum consumption of vanaspati.

Transport Facilities

Transport facilities play a vital role in the development of industries at a particular place. Their role is twofold : (a) in the transportation cost of raw material, fuel, etc., to the factory, and (b) in the cost of transporting finished goods to the markets. For example, in U.P. there are 8 units. Of these, four are at Ghaziabad and one each at Modinagar, Kanpur, Muzaffarnagar and Aligarh. Ghaziabad is ideally situated in respect of transport. It is a railway station and is connected with Calcutta, Amritsar, Pathankot, Dehradun, Bombay and Madras. By road also it is ideally connected. The famous Grand Trunk Road passes through Ghaziabad. Coal, which is required as a fuel, and vegetable oil, which is required as a raw material, can easily be brought by rail at cheap rates. The finished products can be transported either by rail or by road in any direction. Kanpur, which is the largest industrial town of U.P., is a very important railway junction and is also situated on the G.T. Road. It is connected by road with Delhi and Lucknow and with Madhya Pradesh. Thus, this is also an ideal town so far as transport facilities are concerned.

Similarly, Modinagar and Aligarh are also railway stations and are very well connected by road and railway. Aligarh is a railway junction and is connected with Chandausi and Bareilly, Delhi and Calcutta by rail. It is also situated on the G.T. Road. It is very well connected with all important towns situated on this road. Muzaffarnagar and Modinagar are situated on the main railway line from Delhi to Dehradun and are thus directly connected with Amritsar and Delhi by rail. By road also, these are connected with Punjab and through Delhi and Ghaziabad with Calcutta and Madras.

In Maharashtra, there are 10 vanaspati factories of which six are located at Bombay and one each at Chulia, Akola, Amalner, Pachora and Latur. Regarding the position of Bombay, it is too well known to be discussed in detail. The other centres, viz. Akola, Dhulia and Pachora and Amalner, are railway stations and are well connected with roads. These have thus satisfied fully the second important condition for the location of industries, viz. transport facilities in so far as vanaspati industry is concerned.

In Gujarat there are five units which manufacture vanaspati. Two units are situated at Manavadar and one each at Samalaya (Baroda), Bhavnagar and Rakhial. All these units are connected with railway stations and are served by metalled roads which connect them with the national highways and thus can be said to have very satisfactory transport facilities, an essential condition for the location of industry in general and vanaspati industry in particular.

Availability of Manpower

Availability of manpower at reasonable cost is another factor which promotes development of industry—both skilled and unskilled labour is required for the vanaspati industry. In application of this essential condition to the location of vanaspati industry it will be seen that it amply satisfies the manpower condition of the theory of location of the industry. Ghaziabad where four units are established is situated in the heart of the Gangetic plain which is very densely populated. The supply of labour is in abundance. The social and economic conditions of the landless labourers in the villages around the city is none too good and, therefore, they are always interested in getting a job in some factory in Ghaziabad.

As regards skilled workers, these are generally promoted from the unskilled ones and are trained in the factory and whenever there is a vacancy for skilled workers are promoted and in their place mostly unskilled workers recruited. Thus, centres where cheap unskilled labour is available have attracted vanaspati industry along with other industries. Similarly, Kanpur, Aligarh and Muzaffarnagar in U.P. are also urban centres and have ample supply of unskilled labour in their surrounding villages who flock to the towns in search of employment.

The other places in the country where vanaspati manufacturing units have been set up are thickly populated centres and are considered a boon for their rural jobless labourers who, in order to earn a living, flock to cities and are thus easily available for employment for vanaspati units as well.

Accessibility to Markets

The development and growth of vanaspati industry has been in urban areas. For this reason it has been very popular as a cooking medium among the urban people, mainly the educated class who because of not easy availability and unreliability of desi ghee prefer vanaspati for their daily use.

Another important consumer of vanaspati in the urban areas is the 'halwai' (confectioner) who prepares all his sweets in vanaspati and sells them at a comparatively cheaper rate to the urban population. Therefore, the easy market for the vanaspati is the urban centre.

Although raw material-oriented vanaspati industry has been set up especially in the northern region where the market for vanaspati is easily accessible. For example, the factories in Punjab, Delhi, U.P. and Rajasthan are located at places which are ideal for disposal of vanaspati. These are ghee-consuming areas. The price of 'desi' ghee being very high, vanaspati is used as a substitute. Hence, it is in great demand in these areas. Vanaspati produced in West Bengal is easily consumed in the metropolitan city of Calcutta and other urban centres as well as in Bihar and Orissa. It is simply because of easy accessibility to these markets that so many factories have been set up in these areas.

The consumption of vanaspati in the North Zone is the highest in the country. As much as 87.9 per cent of the requirement of the vanaspati is met out of the production of vanaspati in the region. The balance is imported from other States where it is produced in excess of demand. These are West Bengal, Maharashtra etc.

Cheap Motive Power

Before the advent of hydro-electric power all the industries had to be concentrated near and around the coal fields. This fact is particularly true of the industries which require plenty of coal fuel. But with the development of hydro-electric power the necessity of locating industries at or near coal deposits has been obviated. All the places where the vanaspati units have been set up now have cheap electric power in abundance. Some major power projects from which hydro-electric power is being supplied to vanaspati industry are given in Table 3.2.

TABLE 3.2

Generation of Electric Power at Major Power Projects in India and the Recipient States

Name of the Project	Power Generation	State to which power is being supplied
National Projects		
1. Bhakra-Nangal Project (Punjab)	1204000 kw	Punjab, Delhi, Haryana & Rajasthan
2. Damodar Valley Project (Bihar & West Bengal)	628 mw (already consumed)	Bihar, West Bengal up to Calcutta in east and up to Mughalsarai in west.
3. Tungabhadra Project (Andhra & Mysore)	99000 kw	Andhra, Mysore and Tamil Nadu.

In Uttar Pradesh, the following important power generation schemes have augmented the supply of electric power which has helped in feeding vanaspati industry with sufficient power:

	Power	Year
(1) New Thermal Station	64 mw	1967-68
(2) Harduaganj Hydel Scheme	210 mw	1968-69

Further, the places, being linked with railways, the coal supply is also cheaply available to the factories. This is how this great factor which determines the site for location of industries also applies to vanaspati industry.

Banking Facilities

Banking and financial facilities also play a vital role in the industrial growth of a particular place. In fact, banks are the nerve-centre of all business activities. The problem of financing small industries which cater to limited markets is very simple. But the problem of finding finance for large industries is a difficult one. Large capital is required for various purposes, e.g. new industries require money for purchase of land, construction of buildings, purchase and installation of costly machinery.

All the places where the vanaspati factories are established, viz., Bombay, Calcutta, Madras, Delhi, Ghaziabad, Kanpur, etc., were fully developed industrially and commercially even before the first vanaspati factory was set up. Then the industrial magnates and businessmen had surplus money to be invested in new projects. Therefore, there was no problem in so far as raising of capital was concerned, whenever vanaspati production centres were to be set up. But these days even for procuring the working capital which mostly consists of raw materials, banks have to come into help. They play an important role. They advance money for purchase of oil used in the manufacture of vanaspati. In a small town of Ghaziabad there are as many as 16 branches of different commercial banks including that of the State Bank of India.

State Aid

After independence the Government of India declared its industrial policy on 6 April, 1948, promising all necessary help to the industries. For the purpose of financial assistance Industrial Finance Corporations were set up by the Central and State Governments. Import duties were reduced by 10 per cent to 15 per cent on plant and machinery. New industries were exempted from payment of income tax or corporate tax for a period of five years and a chain of laboratories for helping inventions and their application by the industrialists were established.

So far as vanaspati industry was concerned all these facilities were made available to the industrialists who wanted to set up vanaspati manufacturing units at different places.

During recent years there has been a sort of a competition among the State Governments in attracting new industries in their States. For this purpose they repeatedly offer concessions and facilities to the industrialists in the following form:

(1) Ensuring cheaper supply of power for a period of even up to five years.
(2) Facility for loan at very cheap rates.
(3) Tax holiday—the State Governments offer holiday from sales tax or from even state excise duties for a specified period limited to five years.
(4) Promises to lay roads from the site of the factories to the cities.

(5) Even helping in the form of advancing money for starting their factories through their respective Financial Corporations which almost all the States have set up.

The vanaspati factory set up at Rajpura in Punjab and the other at Jhotwara near Jaipur in Rajasthan, have got all the above facilities by the respective State Governments.

Amenities for a Particular Site

The role played by natural amenities in the industrial growth of a particular area is quite important. Physical characteristics such as the level of ground, climate, facilities for the disposal of waste, etc., affect the location of industry. Uneven land is certainly a discouraging factor. On account of this, industrial growth cannot take place in hilly areas or in the plains and in the ravines. Similarly, industry cannot develop in low-level areas where waterlogging is quite usual during the rainy season. Surface with hard ground is best suited for the construction of factories. Vanaspati industry has been located on the plains which is hard and there is no waterlogging.

Social and civil amenities offered by a particular site are also useful. Housing, civic amenities such as light, water, medical facilities, recreation facilities, etc., attract labour. All the places where vanaspati manufacturing units have been located have all such amenities.

Although climate is much more important for agriculture than for manufacturing industry, yet its influence cannot be minimized with regard to location of industry. Extreme climates are injurious to the health of workers and unsuitable to certain industries. Of course, humidity and temperature inside the factories and in the houses of the workers may be controlled through artificial means but that means additional cost and complications. The vanaspati industry is located in areas with moderate climates. The climate at Ghaziabad, Modinagar, Muzaffarnagar, Kanpur, Bombay and Delhi is eminently suitable.

The price of land as available at a particular place also affects the growth of industry there. If the price of land is high the requirements for initial capital increase, and this discourages establishment of factories. Obviously low prices of land attract industrialists. This factor has recently been met by the State Governments by offering land at very low rates. The State Governments themselves are interested in establishing the maximum number of industries so that they are better off economically. All these amenities are available at the places where vanaspati units are set up.

External Economies

By external economies is meant those economies which are enjoyed by a unit on account of widespread development or location of industries in a particular place or region. The facilities are shared equally by all. They have been named as infra-structure in the modern terminology. Several supplementary industries have developed at the centres of vanaspati units. The vegetable oil and container industries are the subsidiary industries of vanaspati. These have been set up at the site of vanaspati industry.

Industrial Peace

Another most important factor which is also taken into consideration by the industrialists these days is the possibility of industrial peace in a particular area. The recent disturbance in the industrial world has brought near chaos in the industry. The industrialists are scared not only to set up new industries but do not even hesitate to shift industries which have been at a place for very long. The extent to which the state of West Bengal had been subjected to industrial turmoil in 1967-68 is evident from Table 3.3.

TABLE 3.3[4]

Stoppages of Work and Loss of man-hours during 1967-68 in West Bengal

Year	Stoppages	No. of Workers involved (in 000)	Mandays lost (in 000)
1967	438	165	5,016
1968	417	263	6,723
1969 (1 January to September)	710	645	8,549

There has recently been a new thinking on planning and setting up of industries. The Government as well as industrialists have begun to feel that there is a great need for some kind of regional planning of industries. This aims at maximization of production and distribution of industrial activity based on broader economic, social and strategical considerations.

In so far as the theoretical aspect of the location of industries is concerned, it is not always entrepreneur who weighs or can weigh the various factors before deciding the place for location of his industry. Of course, mostly the choice of a particular site is governed by his personal interest in the site. In the modern conditions the absence of perfect competition in the widest sense of the term protects an industry from the consequences of a bad location. Vanaspati is also free from extreme competition, and is, therefore, saved from the consequences of bad location.

Thus, in the formulation of a locational policy, it is of utmost importance that the Government should consider first the principles which should govern industrial location and examine distribution of vanaspati industries in the light of these principles.

In the location of vanaspati manufacturing units the tendency of agglomeration has been in operation and deglomeration causes have not yet begun. The factors which have now been responsible for the setting up of additional factories of vanaspati at different places in the country are due to the regional bias which has outweighed the theoretical principles of location of industries.

REFERENCES

1. *Rajya Sabha Debates*, Vol. 69, Unstarred Question No. 1530 answered on 29 August 1969.
2. Registrar General, n. 8, p. 220.
3. *Financial Express*, Bombay, 12 July 1971.
4. P. Thankappan Nair, "West Bengal's Cry of Distress", *Eastern Economist*, New Delhi, 10 July, 1970.

4

Manufacture of Vanaspati

THE MAIN raw materials used in the manufacture of vanaspati are edible vegetable oils. In addition, chemicals such as caustic soda, bleaching earth and filter and nickel catalyst are required for refining these oils.

The following vegetable oils are mainly used for manufacture of vanaspati : (i) groundnut oil, (ii) cottonseed oil, (iii) sesame oil, (iv) soyabean or sunflower oil.

Vegetable Oils

Each oil has its own characteristics and now is equally good for all purposes. Chemical technology has, however, made interchangeability of a large number of oils possible and has increased opportunities for selection of oils.

In fact the Government has now permitted use of various oils which were hitherto not allowed for production of vanaspati. Even mustard oil which has very strong colour and odour was used in the manufacture of vanaspati till 1973, when, due to shortage, its use was prohibited.

For manufacture of vanaspati the main qualities of an oil which are taken into consideration before making a choice in using it in the production of vanaspati are :

Cheapness : The choice of oil used for purposes of manufacturing vanaspati is governed by the price prevailing in the market at the time of its preparation. The cheaper the oil, the cheaper shall be the manufacturing cost and maximum will be the profit.

Refinable Capacity : That oil which is easily refinable is most suited for manufacture of vanaspati. An oil having lower percentage of free fatty acids is easier to refine and, therefore, every factory before purchasing oil under a contract gets the sample of every consignment tested in its laboratory. The consignment is accepted or rejected on the basis of presence of free fatty acids.

Facility of Deodorization : That oil which is easy to deodorize is cheaply hydrogenated and keeps the cost of production low. Cottonseed oil, for example, has got a characteristic odour and a complicated process is required to its deodorization. That is why manufacturers formerly were not prepared to use this oil at all. Now, of course, its use is widespread. With the shortage of groundnut oil, the Government of India has now made it even obligatory on the part of vanaspati manufacturers to use cottonseed oil up to 45 per cent of the total oil used for vanaspati.

Natural Properties : There are certain oils which have some typical properties which render them especially fit to be used for a specific purpose. For example, linseed oil, because of dehydration properties, is best suited for manufacturing of paints, varnishes and inks. If properly refined it can also be converted into vanaspati but it is not used because, firstly, it is not cheaper than the other available oils; secondly, it is more suitable for other uses; and thirdly it does not carry with it any special advantage if turned into vanaspati.

India is the principal producer of groundnut and sesame oils. Table 4.1 shows the production of groundnut and seasame oils in India from 1939-40 to 1949-50 (up to the beginning of the First Five Year Plan) used for manufacture of vanaspati.

TABLE 4.1[1]

Production of Groundnut and Sesame Oils in India from 1939-40 to 1949-50

Year	Groundnut and Sesame Oils (in 000 tons)
1939-40	426.72
1944-45	727.46
1945-46	653.29
1946-47	772.16
1947-48	705.10
1948-49	648.21
1949-50	644.14

From Table 4.1 it appears that during the Second War there was considerable increase in the production of these two vegetable oils in India as the vanaspati industry developed.

Programme of Development

The production of total vegetable oils increased from 11,30,808 tonnes in 1949-50 to 12,92,352 tonnes in 1955-56[2], whereas the total supply of all vegetable oils, including about 1,11,760 tonnes of coconut oil, was expected to be about 14 million tonnes by 1955-56.

Production of vegetable oils in 1950-51 was 12,19,200 tonnes. There were 230 vegetable oil mills registered under the Development and Regulation Act at the end of the Second Five Year Plan whereas the existing power-driven mills were estimated at 3,200.

The estimated production at the end of the First Five Year Plan was 1,78,816[3] thousand tonnes. The target for the Second Five Year Plan was 21,47,830[4] tonnes, but the total production was only 19,71,040 tonnes.

The total crushing capacity of the mills in the country was estimated at 58 lakh tonnes per annum in terms of oilseeds. According to an oil expert in U.P. there were about four lakh village 'ghanies' in India with an annual crushing capacity of about 7.1 lakh tonnes of oilseeds.[5]

Development during Third Five Year Plan

The Total production of all the vegetable oils was expected to be 2.95 million tonnes by 1965-66. But the target could not be reached as oilseed production (revised estimates) of 76 lakh tonnes fell to 62 lakh tonnes due to failure of monsoons and uncertain weather conditions. Though in the initial years of the Third Plan production increased during the last year it dropped to about 183 lakh tonnes.[6] The total production by the end of plan holiday 1968-69 was 85 lakh million tonnes.[7]

Regarding the means for meeting the present shortage of oil the permanent solution lies in increasing the yield of oilseeds in the country and thus bridging the gap between demand and supply. But this is a long-term solution. Meanwhile edible oils will have to be imported from foreign countries to meet the requirements of the country and keep the vanaspati industry alive. At present soyabean oil from the USA and sunflower oil from the USSR are being imported. The terms and conditions of these imports may be reviewed and decisions taken accordingly.

Development During Fourth Five Year Plan

On the basis of growth of population and rise in the standard of living as a result of overall growth rate of Indian economy the Government of India fixed the target of the total oilseeds production at 10.5 million tonnes. This was to be achieved by using both intensive and extensive means of cultivation; extending the area of use of phosphate fertilizers with basal dose of nitrogen as also of plant protection. In addition, the following measures were also taken to raise the productivity rate :

(i) Evolution of drought resistant variety in groundnut, for being grown in under-rainfed conditions;
(ii) Breeding of short duration varieties of groundnut;
(iii) Breeding of pest resistant and tikka (disease) resistant variety of groundnut;
(iv) Development of measures for correcting soil acidity in the eastern region where rainfall conditions are otherwise generally favourable for groundnut cultivation;
(v) Standardization of seed multiplication techniques;
(vi) Intensive research on breeding agronomy, soil and water management diseases and pests and technology of processing soyabean.

During the Fourth Five Year Plan period it was however found that there was a shortfall[8] of 10 lakh tonnes of oilseeds.

From Table 4.2 it would be seen that 1972-73 was the worst year in so far as the five major oilseeds production is concerned. The best year was 1970-71 when the country produced 23,60,500 tonnes of oilseeds.

TABLE 4.2[9]

Year-wise Yield of Five Major Oilseeds in India during the Fourth Five Year Plan

Year	Production of five major oilseeds (in 000 tonnes)
1969-70	2022.3
1970-71	2360.5
1971-72	2292.6
1972-73	1865.0
1973-74	2252.6

The reasons as given by the Minister of Agriculture[10] for this shortfall are listed below :

(i) Efforts made under the Centrally sponsored Development Programme were diffused so that these projects served more as a means of increasing the awareness among the farmers for improved techniques of cultivation rather than creating an impact on production;

(ii) Arrangements for the supply of pure seeds of improved varieties were not adequate;

(iii) In view of low multiplication factor in crops like groundnut, ten new varieties that became available during the middle of the Plan period could not reach the farmer;

(iv) Production technology worked out for groundnut grown under the irrigated and unirrigated areas was yet to be adopted in the field on a large scale;

(v) The major area under the oilseed was rainfed, and since the quality of seed is poor, the plant population in the field was generally low;

(vi) The plant protection programme for pre-seed treatment and protection measures in the early stages of crop growth in the field were not adequate.

Development During Fifth Five Year Plan

It was estimated that by the end of the Fifth Five Year Plan, the country would require about 43 lakh tonnes of vegetable oils for various uses. It was further estimated that the requirement of liquid edible oil would be 23.5 lakh tonnes, Out of this total requirement it was estimated that 8.7 lakh tonnes would be made available from miscellaneous sources, such as cottonseed, rice bran and coconut. The balance of 35 lakh tonnes would have to be extracted from the cultivated oilseeds. To get so much oil, total crop yieldihg 125 lakh tonnes of oilseeds was required.

The Fifth Plan objective was to achieve self-sufficiency in the supply of edible oil. To reach this target, it was decided to increase the annual production of oil seeds at the rate 5.8 per cent per acre. Since the entire growth could not be achieved solely either by raising the productivity level or by bringing additional areas under oilseed cultivation, it was decided to try both the means. The annual growth rate in the total area was fixed at 2.4 per cent and the one in productivity was fixed at 3.4 per cent. This has been shown in Table 4.3.

TABLE 4.3

Targets of Production and Area under Oilseeds on the eve of the Fifth Five Year Plan

Crop	Base Year 1973-74			Target for Fifth Five Year Plan		
	Area (Million hect.)	Yield (Kg./ hect.)	Production (million tonnes)	Area (million hect.)	Yield (Kg/ hect.)	Production (million tonnes)
Groundnut	7.50	800	6.00	8.00	961	7.65
Rapeseed/ Mustard	3.30	576	1.90	3.50	629	2.20
Sesame	2.50	208	0.52	2.70	251	0.65
Linseed	1.70	276	0.47	1.70	288	0.49
Castor	0.40	350	0.14	0.50	160	0.23
Soyabean	0.10	700	0.07	0.43	930	0.40
Sunplant	0.35	857	0.30	0.93	970	0.90
Total	15.85	593	9.40	17.76	707	12.52

Production of Oilseeds in the Past Three Years

During 1977-78, the total production of five major oilseeds was 90.01 lakh tonnes.[11] It rose to 95.54[12] lakh tonnes in 1978-79. There was a rise of 6.1 per cent in the production of oilseeds in the year 1978-79. For the year 1979-80 the official production estimates are not available so far. However, the trade estimates have been published. According to these the total production of the five major oilseeds is likely to be 92.95 lakh tonnes in 1979-80.[13] Thus there is likely to be a short fall of 2.7 per cent compared to 1978-79. But if compared to the production of 1979-80 there is a rise of 12.8 per cent.

Projection of Future Oil Requircments for Various Uses[14]

On the presumption that the population of the country would be 7,052 lakhs by 1986, the demand for vegetable oil for various purposes would be as in Table 4.4 shown.

TABLE 4.4

The various uses for which Vegetable Oils are required.

Requirement of oil for :	(in Lakh tonnes)
1, Vanaspati	10
2. Liquid Oils	20
3. Soap	5
4. Paints and Varnishes	2
5, Other uses	5
6. Exports	3
Total	4.5

(equivalent to 14.65 Lakh tonnes of Oilseeds)

Another 5 lakh tonnes of oilseeds will be required for such purposes as seeds, direct use, and/or export. Thus the oil requirement for Vanaspati would be 100 lakh tonnes.

So far as the Sixth Five Year Plan is concerned a target of 126 lakh tonnes of oilseeds has been fixed.[15] It is expected to yield 35 lakh tonnes of oil. There will thus be a deficit of 265 lakh tonnes of oilseeds. So there is every likelihood of continued shortage of oilseeds supply in the country in the distant future as well, unless these are imported or measures taken already in the direction to raise indigenous oilseeds production in the country to achieve self-sufficiency in oilseeds production are strictly enforced.

In the meanwhile, since oil will have to be imported, it would be better to import oilseeds instead. There will be a lot of saving of precious foreign exchange. India has a substantial capacity of expelling of oilseeds and the cost of extracting oil is very low. Therefore oil extraction can be undertaken more economically in India. This can be explained by an illustration. For meeting a requirment of 1 lakh tonnes of soyabean oil, 10 lakh tonnes of soyabean is required. If the entire quantity of soyabean is imported, it would indirectly be giving a boost to our national economy. It would be providing employment to so many unemployed persons. Although more expenditure will have to be incurred on freight, most of this can be recovered by exporting deoiled meals.

An example can be quoted in this regard. Japan imports majority of world's soyabeans, cottonseed, rapeseed, sesame, sunflower in the form of seed. There, while the demand for deoiled meals for manufacture of cattle feed has grown stupendously, the demand for fats has reached almost the saturation point. Thus Japan is exporting about 20,000 tonnes of vegetable oil to other countries. We should also import seeds and export oils to other countries.

Following recommendations made in 1965 by the study set up by the United Nations on oils and fat industry in Asia and the Far East can still be followed to augment the supply of oil in India.[16]

1. Arrangements should be made to collect and extract oil from about 5.5 lakh tonnes of oil-cakes. It would yield additional oil to the extent of 60,000 tonnes.
2. Stricter control by the Government of India on the use of foodgrain quality solvent by solvent extraction plants should be exercised, so that the Ministry of Health may allow the use of solvent oil as edible oil which is banned today. This will bring forth an additional quantity of about 1 lakh tonnes of edible oils.[17]
3. Use of non-edible oils in the soap industry should be encouraged so as to spare good oils for edible purposes.
4. Better methods of transportation should be established to save a large amount of oil lost by leakage which according to the study group, was as much as 25,000 tonnes valued at $15 million.

Oilseeds Required for Use in Vanaspati Manufacture

Earlier, mostly groundnut oil was used for vanaspati manufacture. The only other oil used by the industry was sesame oil which was statutory requirement to prevent adulteration of vanaspati with desi ghee. Groundnut oil was preferred by the manufacturers of vanaspati because it was available easily and at comparatively cheaper rates. It accounts for 70 per cent of the total production of edible oils in the country. However, it has now lost its place of priority for use in vanaspati. Its use started receding as the crisis in indigenous oilseeds production deepened. It will be clear from Table 4.5.[18]

TABLE 4.5

The Pattern of Use of Different Oils in the Manufacture of Vanaspati

Year	Groundnut	Cottonseed	Sesame	Other	Imported Oil
%	%	%	%	%	%
1966	70	20	5	2.5	2.5
1967	55	20	5	2.5	17.5
1968	67.5	12.5	7.5	2.5	10
1969	50	20	10	2.5	17.5
1970	60	15	7.5	5	12.5
1971	65	10	7.5	5	12.5
1972	60	22.5	5	5	7.5
1973	30	35	7.5	15	12.5
1974	35	40	5	7.5	12.5

From Table 4.5 it will be seen that in 1966 the industry used 70 per cent of groundnut oil for manufacture of vanaspati. This percentage came down to 35 in 1974. In the subsequent years the Government in order to discourage the use of groundnut oil for vanaspati manufacture even fixed its use for this purpose at 25 per cent. The compulsion for resorting to this measure was to save it for making it available for direct use by the consumers.

Despite all these restrictions and shortage, groundnut oil is still being used in the manufacture of vanaspati. A slight fall in the price of groundnut oil encourages vanaspati producers to increase its percentage for use as raw material even beyond the permissible limit. In 1976, when there was a bumper crop of groundnut, the industry defied the statutory obligation of its use and used groundnut oil beyond the 25 per cent because it was available at cheaper rates.

Thus the importance of groundnut oil cannot be minimized in the manufacture of vanaspati.

Production of Groundnut Oil

Table 4.6 gives the production of groundnut and groundnut oil in India from 1950-51 to 1979-80.[19]

TABLE 4.6

Production of Groundnut and Groundnut Oil from 1950-51 to 1979-80

Year	Production of groundnut (in 000 tonnes)	Production of groundnut oil
1950-51	4494.00	780.00
1960-61	6463.00	975.2
1965-66	7698.00	942.5
1970-71	7326.00	1368.4
1975-76	6754.00	1414.0
1976-77	5262.00	1350.0
1977-78	6069.00	1516.3
1978-79	6387.00	1596.75
1979-80 (Trade Estimates)	6400.00	1600.00

From Table 4.6 it will be seen that during three Five Year Plans there has been an over all increase of 88 per cent in the production of groundnut oil. But during the Fourth and Fifth Plans it has fluctuated and fallen. However, from 1977-78 onwards the production in groundnut oil has shown a rising trend.

Though groundnut oil can be used for cooking purposes, it has to be refined for use in margarine manufacture, lubricants, etc., where natural fats are essential. For margarine manufacture the oil undergoes decolorization also.

The most important use of groundnut in India has been in the manufacture of vanaspati since its beginning. Groundnut oil forms the bulk of the raw material used in its manufacture. In 1967 about 3,04,800 tonnes of groundnut oil was consumed by the vanaspati industry.[20] Now it is much less. Sometimes, when there is a shortage, groundnut oil forms only 15 per cent of the total oil used is vanaspati. There are suggestions that the use of groundnut oil for manufacture of vanaspati should be totally banned and instead substitute oils should be used. But looking at the preferences available and the distinct advantages of groundnut oil, banning its use in the manufacture of vanaspati seems impossible.

Sesame Oil

Sesame oil is one of the richest oils and, like other oils, is also used for various purposes. Nearly 75 per cent of its production is used for edible purposes. Hydrogenation takes 8.3 per cent, and 4.2 per cent of the oil is used for the manufacture of paints, pharmaceuticals, insecticides, etc. Its export is totally banned.

It is less perishable as compared to other oils because it contains certain antioxidants which prevent it from becoming stale. It also contains ingredients which can be easily detected by simple chemical tests. It is because of this particular property of sesame oil that it has been made obligatory for the manufacturers of margarine (western countries) and vanaspati to mix a fixed percentage of the oil with them so that these products can be easily tested to find out whether these have been adulterated with desi ghee or butter cream.

Production of Sesame Oil

The production of sesame oil in India has been shown in Table 4.7.[21]

TABLE 4.7

Production of Sesame Oil during Five Year Plans

Years	Production (in 000 tonnes)
1950-51	133.6
1960-61	95.6
1965-66	127.2
1970-71	168.8
1975-76	113.6
1976-77	124.0
1977-78	520.0
1978-79	540.0
1979-80	370.0 Trade Estimates

From Table 4.7 it would be seen that the production of sesame oil is stationary. It rose sufficiently during the years 1977-78 and 1978-79, and, as expected, fell in 1979-80. Rise or fall in the production of this oil, however, is not very material so far as vanaspati industry is concerned because only a limited quantity of this oil is used by the industry.

Cottonseed Oil

Though India is the third largest cottonseed-producing country in the world, yet her cottonseed crushing industry has not developed to any marked extent. The first crushing mill on modern lines was established in the early thirties of this century. This was followed by another in 1937 in Hyderabad (Sind) now in Pakistan.

Almost all the cottonseed crushing mills are located in the States of Gujarat, Maharashtra, Madhya Pradesh, Andhra Pradesh and some in Punjab.

Before the oil is extracted the cottonseed is cleaned, delinted, hulled, and the meats rolled and cooked. The following methods of extraction of oil from cottonseeds are used: (a) Hydraulic pressing, (b) Screw pressing, and (c) Solvent extraction or Filtration extraction.

Development of Cottonseed Oil

It was recommended in the First Five Year Plan to increase production of cottonseed oil by erecting a few plants capable of producing 7,500 tonnes of oil and simultaneously five million pounds of cotton lint. After the Industries Development and Regulation Act, 1951, eight concerns[22] were granted licences during the First Plan period for setting up vegetable oil mills on condition of crushing cottonseed only. These steps were taken to make available cottonseed oil for vanaspati manufacturers which were expected to use this oil in increasing quantities. In addition to the above plants, the Madhya Pradesh Government, under the Second Plan, had a proposal to erect a plant with an actual crushing capacity of 15,240 tonnes of cottonseed.

The total installed capacity of the nine units was 99,771 tonnes of cottonseed per annum. All these units were equipped with delinting and hulling machines. Besides these units cottonseed is crushed by several other mills along with other seeds.

As against the target of an additional capacity of extracting cottonseed oil, envisaged under the Plan, the cottonseed oil was estimated to be about 9,144 tonnes in 1955-56 as compared to about 5,180 tonnes at the commencement of the plan.

A target of 30,480 tonnes of cottonseed oil[23] was proposed for the year 1960-61. There were several problems requiring solution before a scheme of cottonseed oil produetion could be taken in hand, e.g. popularization of consumption of oilcake as animal feed in place of whole seed and disposal of bye-products like cotton linters, etc. The position of cottonseed oil mills in as a whole was reviewed in 1958 by an ad hoc committee on cottonseed oil mills set up by the Government and the target fixed was 60,960 tonnes.[24] Redemption from excise duty gave an impetus to the production of cottonseed oil. Rebate of excise duty payable by vanaspati industry for the use of cottonseed oil was enforced from 1960.

TABLE 4.8[25]

Capacity of Cottonseed Milling in different States

State	Capacity in October 1961 (in tonnes)	Increased capacity after granting licences to more units (in tonnes)
Andhra Pradesh	13066	15240
Tamil Nadu	15240	Nil
Madhya Pradesh	30480	36576
Mysore	54864	44704
Gujarat and Maharashtra	90018	167945
Delhi	Nil	169467
Punjab, Haryana	Nil	9144
Uttar Pradesh	Nil	12192
Total	203668	455268

Taking into account the potential for cottonseed oil extraction and the practical difficulties, production target of 1,01,600 tonnes of cottonseed oil for 1965-66 was fixed.

The production of cottonseed oil in the organized industries rose to 80,000 tonnes (during 1968-69) from a meagre two thousand tonnes during 1952-53. Thus the increase was forty-fold during the course of about a decade and a half.

During the Third Five Year Plan a remarkable increase in the production of cottonseed oil is noticed (Table 4.9) particularly in 1967-68, when it was double of what it was at the beginning of the First Five Year Plan.

TABLE 4.9[26]

Production of Cottonseed Oil in India during 1950-51 to 1973-74

Years	Production (in 000 tonnes)
1950-51	155.0
1960-61	289.0
1965-66	261.2
1966-67	269.5
1967-68	300.5
1968-69	282.2
1969-70	288.9
1970-71	254.3
1971-72	369.6
1972-73	296.4
1973-74	320.8

In August, 1957, the Vanaspati Manufacturers Association of India offered to persuade the vanaspati manufacturers to use cottonseed oil to the extent of 10 per cent of their total oil requirements. This was done to relieve pressure on groundnut oil.[27]

The statutory minimum level usage of cottonseed oil by vanaspati industry was raised to 15 per cent from December, 1972.[28] The Government also encouraged production of cottonseed oil in the country. Through an order, it stipulated that a minimum of 30 per cent of cottonseed oil will be used in the manufacture of vanaspati. In addition various incentives were given to vanaspati manufacturers who used cottonseed oil over and above the stipulated minimum quantity. For example, an excise rebate of Rs. 200 per tonne was allowed if the cottonseed oil was used over and above the prescribed minimum. As a result the industry started making increased use of cottonseed oil. This is clear from Table 4.10.[29]

TABLE 4.10

Quantity of Cottonseed Oil used in Manufacture of Vanaspati

Years	Cottonseed oil used (in tonnes)
1965	34031
1970	92672
1971	76231
1972	135293
1973	153590
1974	123978
1975	175000

However, production of cottonseed oil in India has been very low. If proper planning is done and efforts made its production can be increased remarkably. It would also make possible to increase the supply of vegetable oils to the extent of 2.50 lakh tonnes by the end of the Fifth Five Year Plan.[30] Besides, the pressure on groundnut oil would we reduced.

Soyabean Oil

Soyabean oil appeared on the Indian soil in a large scale as a result of imports from the USA. During 1964 arrangements were made to import 75,000 tonnes of soyabean and cottonseed oil from the USA under PL 480.

In 1965 the Government again imported 1.50 lakh tonnes of soyabean oil from the USA to help the vanaspati industry to steer clear of the crisis of shortage of raw oil for the production of vanaspati. These imports also were made under PL 480.

Because of the rich crop of soyabean and resultant good supply of soyabean oil, it definitely enjoys a price advantage over other oils. In this regard the following remarks of Mr. Glenn L. Pagelar, President of the Soyabean Council of America, are significant : "The United States consumer pays smaller proportion of income for food than any other consumer in the world. What is economic significance of this fact? It means that U.S. consumer has larger amount of income to devote to purchases of other types of products as houses, automobiles, clothing, medicines, etc. Cheap food then generates high demand for other goods and services and so the wheels of economic activity turned more rapidly. Soyabean oil contributes to this economic development because it does exist as a quality oil available in large quantities and at a low price.[31]

On the contrary, in India people spend as much as 65 per cent of their income for purchase of food articles and are left with only 35 per cent of income to be spent on other things. Thus the wheel of economic activities in our country cannot turn so quickly as in America. It is in this context that soyabean oil can play an important role in the development of economic activity in India.

Another advantage of soyabean oil is that it can be used for other purposes, viz. manufacture of soap, varnishes, linoleum, oil cloth and chemicals besides being used as food.

In India soyabean oil has yet to be produced for commercial purposes. Whatever oil used in the manufacture of vanaspati is imported from the USA. There are, however, two snags in producing soyabean in India. These are: (i) the high cost of seed, and (ii) higher rate of seeds required per hectare for cultivation.

Strategy for Soyabean Oil for the Fourth Plan Period

The Food and Agriculture Ministry's projected requirements of edible oil by 1980-81 were estimated to be 357 lakh tonnes. But the Indian National Food Congress held in May, 1970, revised these estimates to 459 lakh tonnes. Although the prospects of imports under PL 480 were extended by three years with the passing of the Agricultural Act 1970 the payment had to be made in dollars. In America also the demand for soyabean oil had increased so there was lesser oil available to be exported to India. What is, therefore, are concerted efforts to augment the internal supply of edible oils. This would also make possible for the country to face up to such a situation.

During the Fourth Five Year Plan period, in order to get 2,00,000 tonnes of soyabean oil, the target set for acreage in 1973-74 was 9,37,500 with the soyabean production of 6,00,000 tonnes. This target if achieved could meet the growing demand due to increase in the population. But it was never achieved.

Caustic Soda

The requirement of caustic soda is not very large. It can be entirely met partly from indigenous manufacturing concerns and partly from imports. These imports are, however, being minimized and it is hoped that in another year or so these will be completely stopped.

Bleaching Earth

In order to decolorize the vegetable oils bleaching earth is used by vanaspati manufacturers. The entire requirements of vanaspati industry are met by indigenous producers. However, when deep-coloured oils like cottonseed oil is processed imported bleaching earth is used because it is stronger and acts more quickly and effectively.

Filter and Nickel Catalyst

This is the most important chemical used in the production of vanaspati. It is used for hydrogenation of oils. Although it also has begun to be produced in the country yet most of the factories use the imported one. The catalyst is generally imported from Holland.

Tin Plates

Besides vegetable oils and chemicals another important raw material which is required by vanaspati manufacturers is tin plates for prefabrication of containers of different sizes to pack vanaspati for sale.

The extent of the importance of tin plates for this industry can be judged from Table 4.11[32] which shows the number of tin containers the industry used during 1955-65. During 1955, 2,79,01,000 tin containers valued at Rs. 2.48 crores, were used. The number shot up to 4,14,00,000 in 1965 valued at Rs. 8.51 crores.

The tin plate supply position had all along been irking for vanaspati manufacturers. The Directorate of Sugar and Vanaspati, Ministry of Food and Agriculture, allotted tin plate quotas to vanaspati manufacturers but these quotas met only two-thirds of their requirements,[32] with the result that the balance requirements were purchased from the open market at exorbitant prices.

TABLE 4.11

The Number of Tin Containers used by Vanaspati Manufacturers during the Period 1955-65

Year	No. of Tin Containers used	Value (in Rs.)
1955	27901145	24829775
1956	34163382	29870628
1957	37225638	39266586
1958	3485172	42752825
1959	34855172	42752825
1960	38898321	42673525
1961	37535615	46792531
1962	50929623	50384571
1963	97917874	57987683
1964	33333081	59691777
1965	41483756	85117186

However, the supply of tin plates had been increasing regularly. The total production of tin plates was 82,000 tonnes in 1960-61. It rose to 1,04,000 tonnes in 1964-65. In spite of this was always shortage of tin plates in the country which was made good by imports from abroad. There had never been an acute shortage of tin plates.

With the introduction of plastic containers the packing in vanaspati has been revolutionized. The plastic containers, though costlier in comparison have become very popular among the users in the country. Moreover the industry does not have to bear the higher cost of the plastic containers. This is charged from the consumers. The consumer also gladly pays more for the empties can be used as lasting containers without threat to the contents.

REFERENCES

1. *Programme of Industrial Development*, 1951-56, Planning Commission, New Delhi, 1967, pp. 263-265.
2. ibid p. 405.
3. *Second Five Year Plan*, Planning Commission, New Delhi, 1962, p. 265.
4. ibid.
5. *Report of the Working Committee for the Formation of Fourth Plan.*
6. *Draft Outline for the Fourth Five Year Plan.*
7. *Draft Fourth Five Year Plan 1969-74*, Planning Commission, New Delhi, p. 184.

8. *Rajya Sabha Debates*, Vol. No. LXXXIII. Answer to Question No. 158, asked on 21-2-1973.
9. "Vanaspati Industry—II—Needless Neglect of Cottonseed Oil", *Financial Express*, 25-2-1975.
10. Rajya Sabha Unstarred Question No. 158 asked on 21-2-73.
11. RBI Bulletin, February, 1980, RBI, Bombay, p. 56
12. ibid.
13. ibid.
14. Base, *Report of the Working Committee for the Formulation of Fourth Five Year Plan.*
15. *Lok Sabha Debates* Sixth Series, (Lok Sabha, New Delhi,) Unstarred Question No. 1653 answered on 24-6-1977.
16. United Nations *Industrial Development in Asia and Far East.* United Nations, New York, 1968, Vol. IV, p. 272.
17. ibid.
18. Adopted from the article "Needless Neglect of Cottonseed Oil" published in the *Financial Express*, 25 July, 1975.
19. *India : A Reference Annual*, 1978-79.
20. *Facts about Vanaspati*, Vanaspati Manufacturers Association, Bombay, p. 21.
21. *RBI Bulletin*, RBI, Bombay, February, 1980, p. 56.
22. *Programme of Industrial Development, 1956-61*, p. 407.
23. *Programme of Industrial Development, 1961-66*, Planning Commission, New Delhi, 1961, p. 671.
24. ibid.
25. ibid.
26. *Rajya Sabha Debates*, Rajya Sabha Secretariat, New Delhi Pt II, Vols. 58 and 69. Unstarred Questions No. 690 and 1730 answered on 5-12-1966, and 29-8-1969, respectively.
27. P.C. n-22
28. *Lok Sabha Debates* Fifth Series Unstarred Question No. 1952 answered on 27-11-1972.
29. B.R. Shah, Role of Cottonseed oil in Vanaspati Industry, Commerce India, 6-9-1975 p. 11-15.
39. Lok Sabha Unstarred Question No. 3701 answered on 15-7-77. *Lok Sabha Debates*, Sixth Series, Vol. No. IV, Question No. 24.
31. Vanaspati Manufacturers Association Reply to Questionnaire issued by the Tariff Commission, 1969, VMA, Bombay.
32. (i) *Directorate of Industrial Statistics Census of Indian Manufacturers (1955-58)*, Directorate of Industrial Statistics, Calcutta.
    (ii) *Annual Survey of Industries, 1960-65*, Central Statistical Organisation, Calcutta.

5

Vanaspati : Production and Consumption

Vanaspati

HAVING BEEN introduced and produced in France first, margarine was soon adopted in other countries of the world. Its production rose sharply from 21,00,000 tonnes in 1938[1] to 46,44,900 tonnes in 1958 and to 63,55,900[2] tonnes in 1967. In India, however, margarine did not become popular because of the general belief that it was manufactured from animal fats for which majority of the Indians have great aversion. The world production figures show the production of margarine rose by 16,91,000 tonnes during a 10-year (1958-1967) period. It was at the rate of 16,910 tonnes per year.

In India Vanaspati is more popular than margarine. The reason is that vanaspati serves as a substitute for ghee which is a very costly commodity and suits the pockets of only the higher middle class. Margarine and other synthetic fats are very popular among the consumers of the world. This is evident from Table 5.1 which shows the production of margarine during 1962-1971.[3]

Table 5.1 shows that the world production of the prepared fats has continuously increased during the period 1962-1971. This also shows the popularity that the synthetic fats have gained during this period in most of the world.

In the Asian region, however, the same trend in the popularity of synthetic fats was noticed.[4]

Table 5.1 shows that among the Asian countries, prepared fats are most popular in Japan, Turkey, Philippines and Iran. These are the least popular in Afghanistan and the Syrian Arab Republic. It also shows that among all the Asian countries its popularity has increased year after year.

TABLE 5.1

World Production of Margarine, Lard and other Prepared Fats during 1962-1971

Year	Production (in tonnes)
1962	5741131
1963	5898507
1964	626699
1965	6409354
1966	6645976
1967	6806656
1968	6960352
1969	7204395
1970	5485684
1971	7628302

In India production of vanaspati began first in 1930 with a very modest quantity of only 303 tons.[5] It rose to 5.21 lakh[6] in 1970 and up to 5.72 lakh tonnes[7] during 1977-78. It, however, fell to only 3.5 lakh tonnes in 1974. Similarly the consumption of vanaspati has also shown a steady increase through this period. It has risen from only 18,000 tons[8] in 1935 to 3.50 lakh tonnes in 1978.[9]

Phenomenal increase in the annual production of vanaspati was recorded during the war time (1939-1946). It rose at the rate of 13,162 tonnes per annum during this period, in the pre-war days the increase was only 2,768 tonnes per annum.

Table 5.3 shows the production of vanaspati before and during the Second War.

The reasons for the sudden spurt in production during the Second World War is attributed to increased purchases of vanaspati by the Government of India for defence personnel.

Even after the end of the war continuous rise in the production of vanaspati in the country although there were setbacks due to various reasons. Production fell by 66.89 per cent in 1948 as compared to that in 1946. There were many reasons for this. Firstly, immediately after partition in 1947 the industry lost a valuable vanaspati market. Former West Punjab, which now forms part of Pakistan, is a ghee-consuming area and vanaspati was consumed in a fairly large quantity in the area. Secondly, communal riots which immediately followed that partition also caused a setback in vanaspati production.

TABLE 5.2

Production of Margarine, Lard and other Prepared Fats in different Asian Countries During the Period 1962-1971

(Production in tonnes.)

Country	1962	1963	1964	1965	1966	1967	1968	1969	1970	1971
Afghanistan**	2400	2400	2500	3500	3400	3100	3000	3000	3000	—
Indonesia*	5700	2600	2009	2071	1316	—	6122	—	10423	—
Iran*	64500	70942	94523	122107	131522	128000	142000	152360	167000	185000
Israel*	14996	15650	16607	16649	18489	20187	22536	23424	25284	28308
Japan§	133000	146000	155000	163000	186000	204000	219000	236000	—	—
Korea*	—	—	—	985	2133	2889	3829	5284	6628	11989
Republic of Philippines	33643	34113	23530	32058	32298	38234	39390	37625	30384	30238
Sri Lanka	—	—	—	3302	3842	3556	1973	1775	4354	4437
Syrian Arab Republic	2885	2081	4418	4595	5774	3911	4018	5700	6500	7300
Turky*	89900	98700	87013	98087	132421	132170	126908	—	—	—

* Margarine only.

** 12 months beginning March of the year stated.

§ Includes crude lard.

TABLE 5.3[10]

Production of Vanaspati and Installed Capacity During the years 1930-46

Year	Production of Vanaspati (in tonnes)	Installed capacity (in tonnes)
1930	303	10000
1935	17363	73800
1937	30207	87970
1938	37943	87970
1940	66709	106270
1945	134749	180800
1946	145000	180800

For many months the factories remained closed. Thirdly, the industry lost a producing unit at Lyallpur (Pakistan) after partition. All these factors brought the production of vanaspati down from 145,000[11] tonnes in 1946 to only 97,160 tonnes in 1948. Another factor which almost created panic among the consumers of this important fat after independence was some misgivings regarding the nutritiousness of vanspati. But all these were temporary setbacks.

From 1951-52 onwards production of vanaspati was controlled in a systematic way by the Planning Commission of India according to its anticipated demand for consumption. The Planning Commission estimated[12] that consumption of vanaspati would be around 3 lakh tonnes at the end of 1955-56 because of increase in population and also because of increased per capita income. Accordingly the Commission fixed the target for annual production capacity at 3,88,900 tonnes. The annual capacity was 3,33,228 in 1950-51 and the total production was 1,70,000 tonnes only.

During the First Five Year Plan

During the First Five Year Plan period both consumption and production of vanaspati increased. While the consumption rose by 78000 tonnes production rose by 90,000 tonnes.

This can be seen from Table 5.4 which shows consumption production and installed capacity of vanaspati during 1951-52 to 1955-56.[13]

TABLE 5.4

Consumption, Production and Installed Capacity of Vanaspati in India during the First Plan Period

Year	Consumption (tonnes)	Production (tonnes)	Installed capacity (tonnes)	Percentage utilisation
1951-52	177000	180000	401100	44.58
1952-53	196000	199000	401100	49.62
1953-54	198000	190000	430000	46.28
1954-55	216000	225000	448400	50.24
1955-56	255000	270000	448400	60.62

It will also be seen that throughout the Plan period the industry always had idle production capacity. The maximum utilization of the total installed capacity was in 1955-56 when 60.62 per cent of the installed capacity was utilized against utilization of 44.58 per cent of the installed capacity in 1951-52. Even during the year of maximum utilization as much as 39.38 per cent of the capacity was idle.

A landmark in the history of vanaspati industry during the First Plan period was its entry in to the international market. Import of vanaspati had altogether stopped during the Second World War. India began exporting vanaspati to various countries in the Middle East and even to the U. K., from where she once imported vegetable oil.

TABLE 5.5[14]

Export of Vanaspati during 1951-52—1955-56

Year	Exports (in tonnes)	Value (in rupees)
1951-52	3100	7530000
1952-53	2800	5790000
1953-54	900	2110000
1954-55	9900	14770000
1955-56	13100	17500000

It will be seen from Table 5.4 that the export shrunk suddenly during 1953-54 but there was sudden increase in the exports during 1954-56 (last two years of the Plan.) The entire fillip in export trade was because of greater demand for this product in the U. K. The industry exploited this opportunity fully.

During the Second Five Year Plan

On the basis of the experience gained during the First Plan period the Planning Commission assumed that the rate of consumption of vanaspati would rise by about 25,000 tonnes per annum and the country would thus require about 380 lakh tonnes of vanaspati for internal consumption in 1960-61. The Commission also estimated that during the Second Plan period the industry might be asked to meet the demand of vanaspati in foreign countries. Accordingly the export target for 20,000 to 25,000 tonnes of vanaspati per year fixed by the Commission.

However, neither consumption nor production of vanaspati went according to the estimates. The increase in production in 1960-61, i.e. the end of the Second Plan. was only about 24.1 per cent compared to that during 1955-56. Table 5.6 depicts production and consumption of vanaspati during the years (1956-57—1960-61).

TABLE 5.6

Consumption, Production and Installed Capacity of Vanaspati during the Second Plan Period

Year	Consumption[15] (in tonnes)	Production[16] (in tonnes)	Annual installed[17] capacity (in tonnes)	Percentage utilized
1956-57	252900	263800	539400	48
1957-58	296000	300100	539400	60
1958-59	296000	299100	540700	60
1959-60	324300	329600	542800	61
1960-61	329300	334900	558800	60

Table 5.6 shows that the overall increases in consumption and production of vanaspati during the Second Plan period was 76,400 tonnes and 71,100 tonnes respectively. Consumption and production turned out to be much below the estimates of the Commission.

The shortfall in production was in fact due to lesser demand of vanaspati within the country and also in the export markets. A redeeming feature of production of vanaspati during the Second Plan period, however, was that there was more utilization of installed capacity. The maximum utilization of installed capacity was done during 1959-60 when 61 per cent of the installed capacity was utilized.

During the Third Five Year Plan

The Planning Commission estimated that the consumption of vanaspati during the Third Plan period would increase rapidly as compared to that during the Second Plan period. According to the estimates of the Commission the consumption of vanaspati would rise to 4,75,000 tonnes[18] by the end of the Third Five Year Plan. This was against the actual total consumption of 3,29,700 tonnes[19] at the end of the Second Plan period. These estimates of consumption of vanaspati in India were drawn up after taking into account growth of population during the Plan period, rise in the per capita income, elasticity of demand and export requirements.

In addition, it was also expected that the vanaspati industry would produce 25,000 to 30,000 tonnes[20] of industrial hard oil in view of the restrictions imposed by the Government of India on the import of mutton tallow. Thus the total production target fixed by the Planning Commission for 1965-66 was 5 lakh tonnes[21] of vanaspati and industrial hard oil.

Production of vanaspati increased by 19.7 per cent during the Third Plan period compared to that in 1960-61. But it did not reach the target during the Third Plan period, as can be seen from Table 5.7.

Contrary to the expectations of the Planning Commission, consumption of vanaspati increased more rapidly during the Second Plan period than during the Third Plan period. It rose by 61,044 tonnes during the Third Plan period whereas it rose by 76,400 tonnes during the Second Plan period.

The utilization of installed capacity rose to 69 per cent during the Third Plan period. This position was better than what it was during the Second Plan period.

On the export front as well the targets could not be reached despite incentives. The groundnut oil prices rose so much in the country that great difficulty was felt in maintaining supply of vanaspati even for internal consumption. The

TABLE 5.7[22]

Consumption, Production and Installed Capacity of Vanaspati during the Third Plan Period

Year	Consumption (in tonnes)	Production (in tonnes)	Annual Capacity (in tonnes)	Percentage utilized
1961-62	336816	341200	558800	61
1962-63	368770	366300	571500	65
1963-64	361608	397600	571500	68
1964-65	422652	365800	591500	63
1965-66	359183	401200	591500	69

Government had to resort to imposition of ban on export of not only vanaspati but also of vegetable oil so that the saved quantity of both these products could be made available for internal consumption. Naturally, exports fell sharply.

Spectacular Progress during Plan Holidays (1966-67 to 1968-69)

For three years 1966-67, 1967-68 and 1968-69 there was no Plan, only annual Plans were drawn up. The production of vanaspati, installed capacity, as also the consumption trend continued to rise during the plan holidays. Production[23] rose from 3.68 lakh tonnes during 1966-67 to 4.76 lakh tonnes during 1968-69. Production during this year rose because there was increased demand of vanaspati for internal consumption[24] which rose from 3.65 lakh tonnes in 1966-67 to 4.70 lakh tonnes in 1968-69. The installed capacity, however, rose by 1 lakh tonnes during a short period of three years. This sudden spurt in the capacity was due to relaxation in the licensing policy announced by the Government of India in 1968.

Thus the progress of industry during the plan holiday period was spectacular.

During the Fourth Five Year Plan

The Vanaspati Manufacturers' Association had drawn up estimates of demand for vanaspati for internal consumption during the Fourth Five Year Plan. These estimates were made after taking into account, as usual, the growth of population and increase in the per capita income. It was estimated that the demand would increase at the rate of

25,000 tonnes per year during the five-year period (1969-74) On the basis of this estimates for the next five years should come to as in Table 5.8.[25]

TABLE 5.8

Year-wise Estimate of Consumption of Vanaspati for the years 1969-74

Year	Estimated Consumption of Vanaspati (in tonnes)
1969	470000
1970	523000
1971	548000
1972	573000
1973	598000
1974	625000

These targets were again not reached during the Fourth Plan Period. This can be seen from the actual production figures of vanaspati during the years 1968-74 (Table 5.9).[26]

TABLE 5.9

Production and Installed Capacity of Vanaspati during the years 1968-73

Year	Production (in tonnes)	Installed Capacity (in tonnes)
1968	474368	635000
1969	482000	700000
1970	521275	1029000
1971	560700	1250000
1972	601300	1250000
1973	464300	1250000

It will be seen from Table 5.9 that the production of vanaspati increased every year from 1968 to 1972. But it dropped in 1973 to 4,64,300 tonnes. The installed capacity rose from 6.35 lakh tonnes in 1968 to 12.50 lakh tonnes in 1972. The industry utilized only about one-third of the installed capacity during 1973.

The above Table 5.9 also shows that production targets were never reached. Of course the annual installed capacity increased out of all proportions—from 6.35 lakh tonnes in 1968 to 12.50 lakh tonnes in 1974. Utilization of installed capacity sharply declined because of this development. It came down to only 45.60 per cent in the year 1971 against the maximum utilization of about 68 per cent during the Third Plan period.

During the Fifth Five Year Plan

The condition of industry further deteriorated partially in 1974-75. Production went down further to 3.53 lakh tonnes. It was lower than even during 1964-65. This is evident from Table 5.10.[27]

TABLE 5.10

Production of Vanaspati during the Years 1974-75, 1978-79

Year	Production	Installed Capacity (in tonnes)
1974-75	353000	1250000[28]
1975-76	500000	1265000
1976-77	540000	1265000
1977-78	572000	1265000
1978-79	600000	1265000

The industry showed some improvement during 1975-76 from the hopeless position of 1974-75. The improvement was not remarkable because the production even during 1977-78 did not reach this figure of 6,01,300 achieved during 1972. The reasons for such hopelessly unsatisfactory performance of the industry are not far to seek. The prices of the main raw material used in the production of vanaspati—vegetable oil—were very high and there was statutory price control in force during 1974-75. The industry could not afford to raise the production of vanaspati and incur continuous loss. The result was the production dropped to the minimum.

The improvement shown in the annual production of vanaspati in the year 1975-76 to 1978-79 was due to the fact that the Government lifted the statutory price control on vanaspati in 1975. The manufacturers were then free to sell vanaspati at a cost which could take into account the rise in the prices of vegetable oils.

The last decade, however, has made an impact on vanaspati industry in India. It witnessed the virtual disappearance of public prejudice against vanaspati consumption—a prejudice which was very common not only in India but in the entire world when one was asked to adopt alternatives in place of traditional items whether in food or transport or in any walk of life.

Whereas during 1960, 85 per cent of the urban population used vanaspati, during 1970 as much as 97 per cent of the urban population was found to be using vanaspati.

Similarly the different uses to which vanaspati is put have also undergone a change during the last 10 years. This can be seen from Table 5.11.

TABLE 5.11

Purposes of Consumption of Vanaspati during the years 1960 and 1979[29]

Purpose	1960 (Urban Group)	1979
1. Spreading	3	41
2. Cooking	28	86
3. Frying	64	91
4. Making sweets	2	74
5. Mixing	—	78

It will be seen from Table 5.11 that whereas the use of vanaspati for the purposes of spreading on the chapati, and mixing in doughs or making of sweets in 1960 was wery small, it is used by a substantial number of persons for these purposes these days. In addition to the abovementioned three main uses of vanaspati its use these days for other purposes has also increased substantially.

Zonal Pattern of Production

In 1968 the entire country was divided statutorily into four zones for the purpose of fixing vanaspati prices although informally these zones had been in existence since 1961. When the statutory price control was imposed the Government decided to review zone-wise progress. These zones are as under:

North Zone: This zone consists of the States of Jammu and Kashmir, Himachal Pradesh, Haryana, Punjab, Rajasthan, Uttar Pradesh and the Union Territory of Delhi and Chandigarh. This zone is primarily ghee-consuming area and as such the demand for vanaspati is quite large.

North Zone's share, at present is more than 51 per cent of the total vanaspati consumption in the country. Naturally the production should be and is also the maximum. The zone is responsible for more than 44 per cent of the total production of vanaspati in the country.

The pattern of production in the North Zone is in accordance with its demand. Out of the total estimated demand of 6.50 lakh tonnes for the entire country, requirement of the North Zone was above 50.8 per cent. The production was also in the same pattern.

South Zone: This zone is made up of the States of Andhra Pradesh, Kerala, Mysore and Tamil Nadu and Pondicherry. except the metropolitan cities of Hyderabad, Madras and Bangalore the entire zone is inhabited by people who are primarily coconut oil consumers. The consumption of vanaspati in this zone is naturally the least. In this zone the demand for vanaspati in 1973-74 was 41,800 tonnes. It was the lowest, only 6.2 per cent of the total requirement. Production in this zone was 52,869 tonnes, i.e. 10.5 per cent.

Eastern Zone: This zone consists of the States of Assam, Bihar, Nagaland, Orissa and West Bengal. This is mainly mustard oil-consuming zone and vanaspati is not so popular. Still, in Calcutta, Bhubaneswar, Patna, etc., the metropolitan cities, vanaspati is quite popular as a cooking medium. There are a few vanaspati producing units also. The demand for vanaspati during 1973-74 was 11,64,000 tonnes constituting 17.8 per cent of the total demand for the entire country. Against this the production of vanaspati in this zone was only 4.1 per cent. Compared to this it was 9.5 per cent or 47,792 tonnes of the total production in the country in 1973-74.

West Zone: This zone comprise the States of Gujarat, Madhya Pradesh and Maharashtra. This is the main groundnut-producing zone and as such groundnut oil has been very popular as a cooking medium. Vanaspati has also become popular because this is manufactured with groundnut oil as its main raw material. In this zone the demand for vanaspati during 1973-74 was 1,35,400 tonnes constituting 20.8 per cent of the whole country's requirement. The production is according to the requirement. It was

1,53,892, tonnes i.e. 30.5 per cent of the total production in the country.

Tables 5.13 and 5.14 show zone-wise production and consumption of vanaspati during 1962-70.

It will be seen from Table 5.16 that the North Zone has all along been the producer of maximum vanaspati in the country. Its production rose upto 44.7 per cent of the total production of the country and consumption escalated up to 51 per cent of the total consumption of the country.

The minimum production was found in the South Zone where the percentage of production ranged between 8.2 and 9 of the total production of the country during the past six years.

Western and Eastern Zones together have been producing 46.3 to 48 per cent of the total vanaspati produced in the country.

Production of vanaspati is concentrated in three metropolitan cities—Bombay, Delhi and Calcutta. These accounted for 63.7 per cent[30] of the total production in India in 1951. The pattern changed in the course of time and after two decades the share of metropolitan cities was reduced to only 27.4 per cent. The reason for such a shift was that during 1971 new units were set up mostly in the areas where vegetable oils were produced so that there could be no difficulty in transportation of these oils.

TABLE 5.12

Distribution of Production Units of Vanaspati according to Installed Capacity

Installed Capacity	No. of Units[31]
30000 tonnes and above	18
15000 tonnes and below 30000	23
10000 tonnes and below 15000	6
5000 tonnes and below 10000	20
Below 5000 tonnes	14
Total	81

Another feature of production of vanaspati in the metropolitan cities was that in 1951, Bombay produced 37.3 per cent of the total production of vanaspati in the countury and Delhi's share was only 13.4 per cent. After two decades this position reversed, while Bombay produced 5.2 per cent, Delhi's share increased to 14.2 per cent. This change in

TABLE 5.13

Regional Pattern of Production of Vanaspati in India : 1962-70

(in tonnes)

Region	1962	1963	1964	1965	1966	1967	1968	1969	1970
Andhra, Madras, Mysore, Kerala	30209	34844	32672	38380	32273	35983	41811	43744	43718
Maharashtra, Gujarat, M.P.	134251	133883	125581	141695	115071	128030	155500	149365	165746
U.P., Punjab, Delhi, Haryana, Rajasthan, J&K	134144	147932	147701	187142	158407	16863[illegible]	205785	215565	234221
West Bengal, Bihar, Assam, Orissa	69581	66166	52021	61545	51476	60306	71263	73596	77599
Total	368885	382825	357975	428762	357227	392956	474359	482270	521275

TABLE 5.14

Regional Pattern of Consumption of Vanaspati in India : 1962-70

(in tonnes)

	1962	1963	1964	1965	1966	1967	1968	1969	1970
Andhra, Madras, Mysore, Kerala	24141	24194	24022	26746	25411	26778	30529	33372	35068
Maharashtra, Gujarat, M.P.	105706	103239	79945	93449	85554	89918	100054	103311	114615
U.P., Punjab, Delhi, Haryana, Rajasthan, J. & K.	147014	147416	166849	194085	164913	185054	231287	242799	249656
West Bengal, Bihar, Assam, Orissa	75545	77617	68832	78745	65464	67008	79106	85450	90132
Supplies to Defence Services	13325	24262	19522	27936	16886	23605	31714	15696	28481
Exports	3039	3999	2498	1683	955	383	515	85	100
Total	368770	380727	361668	422652	359183	392746	473205	480713	518052

TABLE 5.15*

Zonal Pattern of Production of Vanaspati for a Ten-year Period, 1966-1976

(in tonnes)

Zone	1966	1967	1968	1969	1970	1971	1972	1973	1974	1975	1976
Northern Zone	158407	168634	205785	215555	233117	262791	282603	209097	146537	230018	300885
Western Zone	115071	128030	155500	149305	1611457	196383	186165	114124	114124	133297	154355
Eastern Zone	51476	60306	71263	73595	79447	77143	76951	40198	40198	45364	42981
Southern Zone	32273	35986	41811	43744	47254	53857	55226	47430	53246	44748	42981
Total						590172	602245	354105	354105	453477	

*Based on the Annual Report of the Vanaspati Manufacturers Association, Bombay.

Note : Figure in brackets indicate per cent of all-India.

TABLE 5.16

Zonal Pattern of Production and Consumption of Vanaspati for the Five-year Period, 1966-1970

Particulars	Production					Consumption				
	1966	1967	1968	1969	1970	1966	1967	1968	1969	1970
Northern Zone	158407	168634	205785	215565	233117	164913	185054	231287	242799	249747
	(44.3)	(43.00)	(43.5)	(54.1)	(44.7)	(48.2)	(47.1)	(48.9)	(50.2)	(51.0)
Western Zone	115071	128030	155500	149305	161467	85554	89918	100054	103311	107734
	(32.2)	(32.6)	(32.9)	(30.9)	(31.1)	(24.0)	(22.9)	(21.0)	(21.6)	(22.0)
Eastern Zone	51476	60306	71263	73595	79447	65464	67004	79106	85450	90595
	(14.6)	(15.40)	(15.0)	(16.8)	(15.2)	(18.1)	(16.9)	(16.8)	(17.9)	(18.5)
Southern Zone	32273	35986	41811	43744	47254	25411	26778	30529	33372	29382
	(8.9)	(9.0)	(8.6)	(8.2)	(9.0)	(7.0)	(7.0)	(6.4)	(6.9)	(6%)
Export and Defence Supplies	—	—	—	—	—	17841	23988	32229	15771	12242
						(5.0)	(6.1)	(6.9)	(3.4)	(2.5)
Total	357227	392956	474359	482270	521275	359183	392746	473205	480713	489700

the pattern of production of vanaspati was also due to the establishment of more units in Delhi area than in Bombay. It was because Delhi falls into the main consuming area for vanaspati.

Table 5.12 shows that the distribution of installed capacity of vanaspati production has been erratic. On the basis of the installed capacity of the units, more than 50 per cent of them have an annual production capacity of 15,000 tonnes and above. Fourteen units have the capacity to produce below 5,000 tonnes per unit. Twenty units have the capacity to produce between 5,000 and 10,000 tonnes. Table 5.13, 5.14, 5.15 and 5.16 show some regional and zonal patterns of production and consumption of vanaspati.

REFERENCES

1. Humlum Johannes, *Atlas of Economic Geography*, Meiklejohn & Sons Limited, London, W. C. 2, 1947.
2, Growth of World Industry, Vol. II, United Nations 1970, *Commodity Production Data* 1958-1967, p. 58.
3. Growth of World Industry 1971, United Nations, Vol. II, *Commodity Production Data* 1962-1971, pp 101-101.
4. *Growth of World Industry* 1971, United Nations Vol. II, *Commodity Production Data* 1962-1971.
5. Vanaspati Manufacturers Association, *Annual Report 1969* VMA, Bombay, p. 20.
6. *VMA Note* submitted for seminar on Maximisation of Capacity Utilisation and Productivity held in New Delhi on 30-31 August, 1971.
7. ibid.
8. *India-Pakistan Year Book 1948*, Times of India Press, Bombay, p. 863.
9. n. 5.
10. (i) n. 4.
    (ii) Figures in col. 3 from G.D. Binani and T.V. Ramarao, *India at a Glance* Orient Longman's Ltd., Calcutta, 1954, p. 1161.
11. n. 4, p. 20.
12. *Programme of Industrial Development, 1951-56*, Planning Commission, New Delhi, p. 270.
13. (i) n.3, p. 275, (ii) n. 11, p. 418.
    Rajya Sabha Debates, Rajya Sabha Secretariat, New Delhi, 1970, Part 2, Vol. 58, Nos, 13-25, Unstarred Question No. 696 asked on 5-12-1966.
15. n. 3. p. 275.
16. ibid.
17. n. 11, p. 418.
18. n. 11, p. 679.

19. ibid.
20. ibid.
21. ibid.
22. n.3. p. 275.
23. Data calculated on the basis of figures given in the *Annual Reports* of VMA for 1969.
24. ibid.
25. Vanaspati Manufacturers Association *Reply to Questionnaire* issued by the Tariff Commission, 1969.
26. Table I of "Vanaspati Industry—Past Performance" Financial Exports, 24-2-1975.
27. *India : A Reference Annual* 1979, Publication Division, Ministry of Information and Broadcasting, New Delhi, p. 303.
28. Rajya Sabha Unstarred Question No. 449 answered on 21-1-76, *Rajya Sabha Debates, Vol, 94 I & II.*
29. A.K. Deb. "Record Growth of Vanaspati Industry," *Financial Express*, 19 July, 1971.
30. 'Vanaspati Industry—Past two years' Performance and Future Hopes. *Financial Express*, Feb., 1975.
31. Calculated from the information given in a reply in the Rajya Sabha.

6

Capital Management and Labour

As in any other industry both types of capitals, fixed and circulating or working, are required for Vanaspati industry. Fixed capital is required for purchase of land, building, plant, workshop tools, transport equipment and other machineries and fixed assets. Fluctuating or working capital is required for purchase of raw materials and for meeting other day-to-day expenses of the factories, viz. cartage, freight, wages and salaries, office maintenance, other trade expenses, etc.

Previously plant and equipment required for manufacture of vanaspati were imported. Now these are manufactured in the country. The equipment required for vanaspati industry consists of some vessels required for heating, injection of steam treatment under vacuum, etc., filter process and air-conditioning for controlled cooling. For production of hydrogen gas vessels for electrolytic processing are also required. Table 6.1 gives the capital investment in vanaspati industry from 1953 to 1971.[1]

TABLE 6.1

Total Capital Investment in Vanaspati Industry from 1953 to 1971

Year	Capital Investment (in Rs)
1953	130000000
1957	140000000
1961	140000000
1965	190000000
1969	220000000
1971	270000000

From Table 6.1 it would be seen that the investment in vanaspati has doubled in a period of eighteen years (1953-71). The increase was sudden during the period 1961-1965 and 1969-1971 when the investment went up by Rs 5 crores. This was due to the sudden spurt in the number of vanaspati mauufacturing units.

During the year 1974-75, according to the *Annual Survey of Industries*, the total investment in the Vanaspati industry was Rs 40.60 crores. It came down to Rs 39.80 crores in 1975-76. The fall in the capital was due to the fact that the industry has to spend a lesser amount on raw material as the price of vegetable oils which had gone up very high in 1974-75 had come down in 1975-76.

As regards the proportion of fixed and working capitals in the beginning the fixed was larger than the working but later the trend was reversed and, at present, the working capital is about one-third of the total capital investment. This is because during the early period there was lower demand and so lower costs of raw materials, i.e. vegetable oils etc. But with the increase in demand for vanaspati the price of vegetable oils also rose. Hence, increase in the working capital. This will be seen from Table 6.2 which shows distribution of fixed capital investment in the vanaspati industry during 1953-1971.[2]

TABLE 6.2

Working and Fixed Capital invested in Vanaspati Industry in India between 1953 and 1971

Year	Fixed Capital (in rupees)	Working Capital (in rupees)	Total Capital (in rupees)
1953	60000000	70000000	130000000
1957	80000000	60000000	140000000
1961	70000000	70000000	140000000
1965	110000000	80000000	190000000
1971	180000000	90000000	270000000

During 1974-75 and 1975-76 the fixed capital investment in the industry was Rs. 20.45 crores and Rs. 22.35 crores respectively. On the other hand the working capital during these two years was Rs. 20.15 crores and 17.45 crores respectively. The reasons for fall in the working capital, as said above, were fall in the price of raw materials, and vegetable oils. During the year 1957 there was a rise in the fixed capital but a fall in the working capital.

As regard the source of money for investment in the industry, earlier only individual entrepreneurs invested the money. Later, when the banking system strengthened in the country, the investment from banks became popular.

Commercial banks have always been the best source of financing vanaspati manufacturers. But due to rise in the prices of vegetable oils the Reserve Bank of India imposed restrictions on the financial credit to check the rise in price. Vanaspati manufacturers have been able to procure loans in quite large amounts to finance the units depending upon their relations with the banks. But restrictions imposed by the Reserve Bank of India from time to time on the advances by the commercial banks to the vanaspati manufacturers have put some curbs on these sources of finances for the vanaspati manufacturing units. Earlier the Reserve Bank of India imposed restrictions on the margin of advances against the security of oilseeds but since 1964 vegetable oils and vanaspati stocks have also been made subject to restrictions on advances by commercial banks. The Reserve Bank of India issues orders from time to time for credit control thereby restricting or relaxing advances against the vegetable oils and/or vanaspati.

The industry has all types of management. Some of the units are part of the big multinational corners. Others are registered as joint stock companies. There are still others which are under the management of private limited companies. They are also in the public sector.

In the country there are only four units in the public sector. Of these, the one, Government Hydrogenation Factory at Kozhikode (Kerala), was set up by the Kerala Government. The other three—Ganesh Flour Mills at Kanpur and at Delhi and the Amritsar Oil Works at Amritsar—were taken over by the Government as these units were declared sick and the private managements were playing truant with the government. The total production capacity of these four units is 84,000 tonnes. The rest of the units are in the private sector.

Labour

From the point of view of labour vanaspati industry is very important. It provides on an average daily direct employment to about 10,000 to 15,000 people 3,4. In addition approximately 60,000 people are indirectly employed. This figure does not include those working in the field for growing oilseeds, the main raw material for vanaspati manufacturers.

As per the international standard classification of occupation recommended by the ILO, workers in vanaspati industry can be classified into the following categories ;

(a) Professional, technical and related personnel.
(b) Administrative, executive and managerial personnel.
(c) Clerical and related workers (including supervisors).
(d) Production and related workers (including supervisors).
(e) Watch and Ward and other services.

Table 6.3 shows distribution among different categories of workers in a vanaspati unit.

TABLE 6.3

Percentage of Different Categories of Workers Required in Vanaspati Industry[5]

Categories	Percentage
Professional related personnel	3.9
Administrative, executive and other managerial Personnel	1.0
Clerical and other related workers	9.4
Production and other related workers	78.4
Watch & Ward and other services	7.3
Total	100.00

Table 6.3 shows that, as natural in a vanaspati unit, the maximum percentage of the production related workers.

In this industry women workers are not very common. There are, in all, about 206 women workers employed in the industry. No woman worker is engaged in the production process directly. In most of the cases the women are engaged as unskilled workers and are required to do jobs like loading and unloading, cleaning of groundnuts, bringing coal to the boiler house, feeding machines with raw material and in scavenging work.

There is no child labour engaged in the industry.

System of Recruitment

Direct recruitment is the most common mode of recruitment in vanaspati industry. In most of the cases appointment of a worker is made from among those who gether at the gate of the factory. Recruitment is also made by means of advertisement and through personal contacts.

Because of insistence of the Government to recruit workers through employment exchanges, recruitment of workers at the gate is declining.

In vanaspati industry absenteeism is not a problem. Still it is there. Among the big concerns like Hindustan Lever there is only one per cent absenteeism. The industry like any other industry in the country is not free from labour trouble. During 1971 there were four disputes in the country where 1,421 workers were involved and this dispute resulted in a total loss of 11,000 man-hours. But in 1972 the number of disputes was reduced to two and the total number of workers involved in these disputes was 370. The total man-hours lost were 5,000. But in the year 1973 the number of disputes rose to 14, the number of workers involved also rose to 4,065. The total number of man-hours lost was 96,000.[6]

As regards trade union movement in Vanaspati industry it has made definite inroads into this industry as well. As many as 70 per cent of workers of vanaspati industry have organized themselves into trade unions. During a period of 10 years (1961-1971) the number of trade unions having membership on the vanaspati industry has come down from 13 to 10. The membership, however, went up from 2,000 in 1961 to 3,000 in 1971. Thus about one-fourth of the total average daily workers in this industry are members of trade unions. But there is less rivalry among trade unions in the vanaspati industry.

As per national industrial classification there were six unions with a membership of 1,000 in 1971.[7] There was no change in the membership in the following year. This number is not much.

REFERENCES

1. Compiled from : (i) 1953-58—*Census of Indian Manufacturers* Directorate of Industrial Statistics, Calcutta; (ii) CSO Annual Survey of Industries, Central Statistical Organisation, Calcutta.
2. ibid.
3. *Times of India Directory 1979*, Times of India, Bombay, pp. 60-61.
4. *Indian Labour Statistics 1975*, Labour Bureau Department of Labour and Employment, Government of India, Simla.
5. *Survey Report of Labour Conditions in Hydrogenated Oil Factories in India 1965-66*, Manager, Government of India Press, New Delhi, 1969.
6. *Indian Labour Statistics*, 1975.
7. ibid., Table 6.2 (c), pp. 184-185.

7

Economics of the Industry

Cost Structure

VANASPATI, next to sugar, is the most important food industry, and is used in the kitchens of the rich and the poor alike. Any increase in its price as a result of a rise in its cost of production affects the consumer and any decrease in its price gives relief to the common man.

Conversion of vegetable oil into hydrogenated fat (vanaspati) is a chemical process and as such, has been argued that it should be treated as a chemical industry. Also that vanaspati industry should be subject to the economics of scale as other chemical industries are. But it is not so. The reason is that for the manufacture of vanaspati the raw material component of the total cost is very high. This is not so in the case of other chemical industries. In the process of manufacture of vanaspati, according to the Tariff Commission, only five per cent value is added to the finished product.

For calculating the cost of production of vanaspati the entire process has been divided into the following heads by the Tariff Commission: Processing, Selling and Distribution, Packing, Freight and Return.

According to the Commission most of the expenditure is incurred under two heads, viz. 'processing' and 'packing', which account for 79.90 per cent of the total expenditure. The remaining 20.10 per cent is accounted for towards 'selling' and 'distribution', 'freight' and 'return of the investment'. Thus, for calculating the cost of vanaspati, the main expenditure is towards the cost of raw material, i.e. the vegetable oil. This expenditure is fluctuating because it is depending upon the price and availability of the vegetable oil in the market. If the vegetable oil is available or made available by the Government at cheaper rates, the cost of production goes down. On the hand if, because of short supply or delay in the import of oil, the prices of vegetable oils rise, the cost of production of vanaspati automatically rises.

The processing of vegetable oils itself is made up of several stages and for calculating the cost of production of vanaspati, cost of each stage has to be calculated. The following are the various stages of processing vegetable oil into vanaspati: Refining of the raw oil, Hydrogen generation, Hydrogenation, Cooling and Salaries and Wages.

The cost of each of the above stages has been calculated in order to find out the overall cost of production of vanaspati.

Refining of Raw Oil

The first stage is of refining the raw vegetable oil. The cost of refining a raw vegetable oil depends upon the quality of the vegetable oil. For purposes of calculation, refining of one tonne of vegetable oil has been taken. For refining oil some steam is required for driving the agitators and pumps. In addition two chemicals—caustic soda and bleaching earth—are also required. If the cost of each of these items is added then the cost of refining one tonne of oil can be found. (For driving the agitators and pumps 2,640 lbs. of steam is required which is equated to 60 kgs. of coal. The prevailing cost of 60 kgs. of coal will give us the cost of 2,640 lbs of steam. Or it requires 33 units of electricity to drive the agitators and pumps. The cost of electricity at the current rates has to be calculated and added. The cost of caustic soda and bleaching earth is also added).

Hydrogen Generation

The next stage of manufacture of vanaspati after refining of oil is hydrogenation. For this hydrogen has to be generated first. Vanaspati manufacturers use an electrolytic process for hydrogen generation. The other process is iron-steam-contact process which is cheaper. This process is not very popular as this contains impurities. Therefore, the first method is mostly used by the manufacturers of vanaspati.

For hydrogen generation also cost has to be calculated by calculating the cost of various components required for the generation of hydrogen. It has been accepted that for hydrogenation of one tonne of oil 1,600 cu.ft. of hydrogen gas is required. So the cost of hydrogenation of one tonne of oil will be the same as that of generation of 1,600 cu.ft. of hydrogen gas. For this purpose two things—electric energy and steam for making distilled water—are required. For 1,600 cu.ft. of hydrogen gas about 200 units of electric energy is required. The cost of 200 units of electric power at the current rates will give us the total cost of the electric energy for production of 1,600 cu.ft. of hydrogen gas.

As regards the distilled water, on inquiry it has been found that for generation of 1,600 cu.ft. of hydrogen gas 10,000 gallons of distilled water is required. For distilling 10,000 gallons of water 10.6 kg. of coal is required. Thus the cost of 10.6 kg. of coal would give us the cost of distilling 10,000 gallons of water required for one tonne of vanaspati.

Hydrogenation

Hydrogenation or hardening proper is a separate process in itself. It requires steam, electric power, catalyst for completion of the process. For hydrogenation of one tonne of vegetable oil 1,320 lbs. of steam is required and 10 kgs. of coal is needed and a total of 38.8 units of electric energy will be needed for driving motors. Catalyst is an imported item. Now, approximately worth Rs. 44 is required for this process. Thus the total cost of hydrogenation of one tonne of vegetable oil, will be the total of the cost of oil, of 10 kgs. of coal, 38.8 units of electric power and Rs. 44, i.e. the cost of the catalyst. Minor expenditure on lubricating material for the hydrogenation plant which is negligible should also be added.

Cooling

The third stage of vanaspati manufacture is cooling. This is also done through various plants consisting of compressors, agitators, etc. The cost of cooling operation is made up of the cost of oil, electric power for running motors and agitators, compressors, cooling plants, lubricating and cleaning material. The total cost in respect of all these items comes to Rs. 12

only. In this cost, the cost of huge quantity of water required is also included.

Salaries and Wages

A vanaspati factory with 100-tonne-per-day capacity and producing either to its capacity or between 75 and 88 tonnes per day requires 13 officers, 53 clerical and technical staff including those in the accounts departments, 17 supervisors, 83 peons and watch and ward, 351 workers—both skilled and unskilled—and 25 persons for the sales department. The monthly bill of these members of the staff of the factory is as under :

Particulars	*Amount*
Officers	Rs. 25,990
Clerical, technical and accounts deptt. staff	16,953
Supervisors	7,566
Watch & Ward & Peons	12,364
Refinery staff	8,710
Packing	5,308
Soap Department	2,473
Workers (Regular)	18,410
Substitutes	4,333
Groundnut oil loading and unloading	3,771
Sales Department	7,749
Others	4,373
Total	1,18,000

The manufacturers have to pay commission to the wholesalers and other distributors. The manufacturers also pay rebate to wholesalers whenever there was a statutory revision of vanaspati prices. These items cost approximately Rs. 60 per tonne.

Depreciation on Plant and Machinery and Building

The cost of vanaspati plant of 25-tonne-per-day capacity was about Rs. 4,50,000 in pre-war days but now it costs Rs. 12 lakhs. These days 25-tonne-per-day capacity plants are uneconomic. Most of the vanaspati factories have installed 75 tonne-per-day capacity plants which cost Rs. 1 crore.

The installation of a vanaspati factory equipped with all auxiliary machines now involves an expenditure of Rs. 1.25 crores including a moderate working capital.

If the plant and machinery are worth Rs. 1 crore the depreciation at the rate of 75 per cent per annum comes to Rs. 7.50 lakhs.

Thus the total amount of Rs. 1,13,00,000 can be accounted towards the expenditure on land, building and machinery. The total depreciation for these two items for one year would amount to Rs. 78,000. The cost of these two items for one day would be Rs. 78,000÷300=Rs. 2600. (This cost is on the presumption that the factory is producing 75 tonnes of Vanaspati per day and is run for 300 days in a year). The cost of land and building for producing one tonne of Vanaspati would be Rs. 2,600÷75=Rs. 34.33. To this amount we may add amount towards interest on capital. Thus the total cost of production of one tonne of Vanaspati for towards land, building and capital would come to Rs. 50.11.

The cost of labour for producing one tonne of vanaspati would equal to Rs. 62.90 (This cost has been calculated on the presumption that the plant is producing 75 tonnes of vanaspati per day and the factory has worked for 25 days in a month).

But if the foctory is producing to its capacity, viz. 100 tonnes per day, the cost of labour would be only Rs. 47 per tonne. Therefore, it is always profitable that the factory should be run in such a manner as the maximum utilization of plant may be achieved.

Additional Expenditure Packaging

Regarding packaging per tonne of vanaspati for sale in the market only Rs. 273 is allowed. This amount has recently been agreed to by the Government. During the year 1968 because of the strike in the Hindustan Steel Ltd. and the Rourkela Steel Plant the prices of tin plates shot up. The industry had to pay more for purchase of tin plates for their requirements. The packing expenses allowed during these days were Rs. 229 only which grew very uneconomic. The Government ultimately agreed and fixed the packing charges at Rs. 273.

Many units have their own fabrication units but others get them fabricated while some others purchase them from the fabricators. These packing expenses are covered if the manufacturers get tin plates as control rates but if they have to purchase in the open market they have to pay more and the expenses on packing are more than Rs. 273 (allowed by the Government). These days, however, there is no shortage of tin plates in the country and the expenditure of Rs. 273 allowed by the Government is sufficient to cover the packing expenditure for one tonne of vanaspati. The expenditure on bigger packs is slightly less.

Distribution Rebate and Commission

For distribution of vanaspati the manufacturers have to spend money on transport of vanaspati to different places for the wholesalers etc. The distribution is done by means of rail, road transport, bullockcarts and even by hand. In addition, manufacturers use their own means of transport on which they have to spend money initially for acqiuring them.

Before the price control on vanaspati was lifted the total cost of production excluding of oil used of one tonne of vanaspati was calculated as under:

	Rupees
Refining—pre- and post-hydrogenation	39.35
Hydrogen generation	42.00
Hydrogenation	54.85
Cooling expenses	12.00
Salaries and wages	62 90
Packing and distribution	273.00
Transport	60.00
Depreciation and interest on capital	50.11
Profit including taxes and dividends	33.79
Total	628.00

The cost of oil comprises 80 per cent of the total cost of vanaspati. The prices of vegetable oil fluctuate. The Government used to fix prices of vanaspati on the basis of fluctuations in the prices of edible oil. It used to calculate the cost of vegetable oil on the following basis :

(a) weighted average cost of oil purchased by factories in

each zone during the fortnights, 1 to 15 and 16 to the end of the month; and

(b) delivered cost of soyabean oil/sunflower oil supplied by the Government of India at lower rates in such proportions as Government deemed fit for each pricing period.

These were true when the price control on vanaspati industry was statutorily applicable but since January, 1975, the price control has been lifted and the manufacturers fix the prices of vanaspati themselves. These prices fluctuate with the prices of vegetable oils.

8

Vanaspati and Consumer

VANASPATI is used by the people in India as a substitute for ghee just as margarine is used by the Western people as a substitute for butter. Vanaspati user belongs to that strata of society which is above the poverty line. Indians use vanaspati for the following purposes: spreading, cooking, frying, preparing sweets and mixing.

During the earliest days of vanaspati industry the use of vanaspati was confined to the people of very low income who could not afford desi ghee. Later, the popularity of vanaspati increased and its consumption rose considcrably. This can be seen from Table 8.1 which shows the sale of vanaspati during the years 1935-1946.[1]

TABLE 8.1
Sale of Vanaspati in India during 1935-1946

Year	Sale (in tonnes)
1935	18000
1936	22000
1937	32000
1938	40000
1939	51000
1940	65000
1941	84000
1942	71000
1943	87000
1944	103000
1945	143000
1946	137000

It will be seen from Table 8.1 that consumption of vanaspati rose from 18,000 tonnes in 1935 to 1,37,000 tonnes in 1946 (and to about 5.50 lakh tonnes in 1976).

The Planning Commission estimated[2] that by the end of 1955-56 the consumption of vanaspati would be around 3 lakh tonnes.

The consumption of vanaspati increased during the First Plan period from 1.77 lakh tonnes in 1951-52 to 2.55 lakh tonnes in 1955-56.[3] It, however, fell short of the estimate of the Planning Commission. At the end of the Second Plan period it rose to 3,29,300 tonnes.[4] During the Third Plan period it, however, did not rise at the rate at which it rose during the first two Plans. During 1965-66 the consumption of vanaspati increased to 3,59,183.[5] The annual consumption during the Second Plan was 15,280 tonnes. As against this the average annual consumption of vanaspati during the Third Plan period was 4,473 tonnes.

During the three years after the Third Plan, 1966-67 to 1968-69, the consumption of vanaspati rose from 3.65 lakh tonnes in 1966-67 to 4.70 lakh tonnes in 1968-69.

During the period 1971-73 the consumption declined from 5,18,052 tonnes to 4,71,697 tonnes.[6]

The year 1974 was the worst year from the point of view of the consumer. The production of vanaspati dropped to 3,54,105 tonnes and the harassed consumer had to pay more than the statutorily controlled price. As a result the consumption came down.[7] Thus, during this year, vanaspati was used only by that class of the society which could afford to pay more and purchase it in the black market.

In 1973-74 the Vanaspati Manufacturers Association (VMA) had estimated that the consumption of vanaspati would rise at the rate of 25,000 tonnes per year. They had estimated that in 1976, 7,33,000[8] tonnes of vanaspati would be consumed. It, however, did not happen. Only 5,50,780[9] tonnes of vanaspati was consumed in 1976.

Table 8.2 shows region-wise consumption of vanaspati for 1966-1976.

From Table 8.2 it would be seen that on account of increase in the population and rise in the standard of living the consumption rose, in eleven years' time, by 45.8 per cent in

TABLE 8.2
Regional Pattern of Consumption of Vanaspati[10] for the period 1966-1976

Year	Zone				
	Northern	Western	Eastern (in tonnes)	Southern	Export and Defence
1966	164913	85554	65464	25411	17841
1967	185054	89918	67008	26778	23988
1968	231287	100054	79106	30529	32229
1969	242799	103311	85450	33372	15781
1970	249747	107734	90595	29382	12242
1971	249656	114615	90132	35068	28581
1972	313879	122832	103240	40476	21975
1973	228257	105149	75994	39552	22745
1974	175272	72161	58586	36386	14338
1975	240516	87238	72702	34522	39980
1976	305021	102203	82848	39980	20736

North Zone and by 16.29 per cent in West Zone, by 20.98 per cent in the East Zone and by 36.44 per cent in the South Zone.

The maximum rise was in the North zone. It was because during this period the standard of living of the inhabitants of this zone rose due to the 'green revolution'.

Another thing that is evident from the Table 8.2 is that in 1974 the production fell suddenly. This was because during this period the industry passed through a serious crisis due to the exorbitant rise in the price of raw material, i.e. vegetable oil and the statutory price control.

As regards the pattern of consumption of vanaspati the people of states which are traditionally ghee-consuming States consume maximum quantity of vanaspati. The States of Punjab, Haryana, Rajasthan, Delhi, Uttar Pradesh consume 50 per cent of the total vanaspati consumed in the country. The two metropolitan cities of Bombay and Calcutta account for 10 per cent each and the remaining 30 per cent is consumed by the rest of the country.

It will be seen from Table 8.3 that the North Zone which is made up of the States of Punjab, Haryana, Rajasthan, U.P. etc., consumed 55.45 per cent of the total vanaspati consumed in the country.

TABLE 8.3
Zonal Distribution of Percentage Consumption of Vanaspati

Zone	Percentage of the total consumption
Northern	55.6
Western	18.5
Eastern	15.2
Southern	7.3
Export and Defence	3.4

The Western Zone's share is only 18.5 per cent. This is because people in this Zone prefer groundnut oil unrefined to hydrogenated oil or vanaspati. In the East Zone the main medium of frying cooking is mustard oil that is why the region consumes only 15.2 per cent. The Southern Zone consumes only 7.3 per cent. This is due to the reason that in this region the main medium of frying and cooking is coconut oil. This pattern still exists though with slight marginal modifications.

Nutrition and Vanaspati

From the point of view of consumer the most important reason for consumption of vanaspati, or for that matter any other fat, is its nutritive value. Every government keeps the health of its nation in view whenever the question of permitting a new consumable article comes up. In the Western countries where the synthetic fats were introduced first, the Governments concerned were apprehensive in the beginning.

Margarine was subjected to severe restrictive legislation in the U.S.A. and in other countries. The Oleomargarine Act 1886[1] enforced by the U. S. Administration contains these restrictions, in detail. The U. S. Government imposed prohibitive tax on yellow margarine, levied high licence fees on all manufacturers, wholesalers and retailers of the product and in all respects subjected it to various other restrictions. The object was only to prevent yellow margarine from reaching its normal consumption level but to prevent its sale for a long time also. This was because in appearance it looked like butter. Later the U. S. Administration thought that the manufacture of margarine although not harmful was not in their national interest. There was, therefore, a wave of several legislations through which production of yellow margarine was highly restricted.

It was only after the manufacturers of margarine enriched it with vitamins A and D and when the Government was satisfied about the whole'someness of the product that the restrictions on the manufacturer of margarine were withdrawn/ relaxed. These days there are no restrictions on the manufacturers of margarine in the USA and Western countries. Indian consumer is, however, still not fully convinced of the nutrition value of vanaspati. There is a sizable proportion of population especially in the Northern region, which is of the view that vanaspati is injurious to health. These people still prefer to go without fats rather than using vanaspati for frying and cooking their food. On the other hand there is another class of people which believes that scientifically there is nothing in vanaspati and that goes to prove the presumption that vanaspati lacks in nutritive value. The majority of people in India believe that vanaspati has no minus point from the point of view of consumer. For judging whether vanaspati fat is nutritious or not, the most important yardstick is to examine its digestibility.

This has been done in detail from time to time in India and abroad.[11]

A report containing the damaging effects of vanaspati consumption was published in 1947 by M/s A.K. Ray and A.K. Pal[12] who were working in the Indian Veterinary Research Institute, Izatnagar. This was so alarming that Dr. Rajendra Prasad, the then Food Minister, immediately ordered a comprehensive study by the scientists. He was even prepared to ban production of vanaspati if there was the slightest doubt about its nutritive value. To safeguard the interests of consumers two separate committees were set up by the Government of India. One was set up by the Food Department and the other by the Council of Industrial and Scientific Research. These Committees examined it carefully. The apprehensions of M/s Ray and Pal were proved to be incorrect by both these committees.

In order to determine whether vanaspati has nutritive value or not the nutritive value of the raw material which is used in manufacturing vanaspati has to be found out. Since vanaspati consists of 95 per cent of vegetable oil and five per cent of sesame oil, nutritive values of these oils should first be found out. First of all digestibility of these oils will have to be found out. The main oil used is groundnut oil. Hence digestibility of vanaspati was dependent on the digestibility of groundnut oil. The melting point of groundnut and sesame oils is 37°C.[13] The melting point of vanaspati is thus the same as that of its raw oil, i.e. 37°C. The Government of India has prohibited the use of vanaspati as 'edible ghee' if it does not have its melting point at 37°C. This has been put at this degree because it is almost identical with the human body's temperature (a product is easily digested and assimilated in the body which has the same melting point as that of human body). If it is otherwise it is injurious to the health of the consumer.

When the question of nutritive value of vanaspati for its consumers came up for discussion in the Lok Sabha in 1954 the then Health Minister, Shri D.P. Karmarker, placed the finding of the Indian Council of Medical Research before the House. These were :

> The effects of hydrogenated oils have been studied in detail. As a result of these studies it has shown that vegetable oils like groundnut oil, sesame oil and their hydrogenated products with melting point 37°C and butter have almost the same nutritive value. Hydrogenated oils have similar digestibility as non-hydrogenated oils. The hydrogenated oils influence the utilisation of other dietary constituents such as calcium to the same extent as untreated vegetable oils and butter. However, butter and hydrogenated fats as sold in India are good source of Vitamin 'A'.

The above finding of the ICMR shows that the consumers' health is not hampered by the consumption of vanaspati. On the contrary there is an additional advantage, that is, vanaspati is fortified with Vitamins 'A' and 'D'. To protect the interest of the consumers the Government of India has made it obligatory on the part of the manufacturers to add Vitamin 'A' at the time of manufacturing vanaspati. But Vitamin 'D' is optional for the manufacturers. However, Vitamin 'D' is invariably added to vanaspati by every manufacturer. Thus vanaspati is more nutritive than even the 'desi' ghee (of cow) which is richer in Vitamin 'A'. This is because Vitamin 'A' is not that stable in ghee as in vanaspati. In addition, vanaspati is enriched with Vitamin 'D' making it more nutritive.

Experiments and tests have shown that vanaspati is not at all harmful even after application of heat which is inevitable while cooking or frying with it. There is another plus point which vanaspati has from the point of view of consumers. In storing and in heating there is a loss of Vitamin 'A' in both Vanaspati ghee. But in the case of vanaspati the extent of loss is lesser than in the case of ghee. Thus the present position regarding the consumption of vanaspati is that it has been accepted as a main medium for frying and cooking in India. This has set at rest the controversy about its nutritive value. Everyone, rich or poor, now accepts it as an essential article of consumption.

REFERENCES

1. *The India and Pakistan Year Book 1948*, Times of India Press, Bombay, pp. 863-64.
2. *Programme of Industrial Development 1951-56*, Planning Commission, New Delhi, p. 270.
3. *Industrial Development in Asia and Far East*, United Nations, New York, 1966, Vol IV, p. 275.
4. ibid. 275
5. ibid. 275.
6. *Annual Report of Vanaspati Manufacturers Association of India for the year 1971-1973.*
7. ibid., 1974.
8. VMA *Reply to Questionnaire* issued by the Tariff Commission.
9. VMA *Annual Report* for 1976.
10. *Annual Reports* of VMA for the years 1966-1976, VMA, Bombay.
11. H.J. Desai, *The Lipids*, Vols. I & II, Terscence Publishers Inc., New York, 1950 and 1965 respectively.
12. S.N. Ray and A.K. Pal, *Science and Culture*, 1947, p. 496.
13. G.S, Hattangadi, *The Vanaspati Industry*, The Indian Central Oil Seeds Committee, Bombay, 1958, p. 49.

9

Colouring of Vanaspati

AFTER THE doubts about the nutritive value of vanaspati cleared the most important thing that agitated the minds of the Government, the leaders, and the public was to prevent the unsocial elements from using it as an adulterant with the 'desi' or 'pure' ghee. In the thirties when vanaspati was imported from Holland it was soley used for adulterating it with 'desi' ghee. This vice attracted repeated discussions in Parliament. As early as in 1949 a question was raised in the Constitutent Assembly[1]. During the course of discussions colouring of vanaspati was suggested by legislators and other members of the public to prevent it from being misused as an adulterant.

Before we go to the question of colouring of vanaspati, let us first examine how the Western countries, who faced a similar problem when margarine was introduced, tackled it. These Governments made it obligatory on the part of the manufacturers to add sesame oil when manufacturing margarine.

The Government of India followed the lead and a notification[2] was issued in 1947 making it compulsory on the part of vanaspati manufacturers to add five per cent sesame oil when manufacturing vanaspati. The Western countries had not done this. The relevant notification reads as follows :

> Vanaspati shall contain raw or refined sesame oil not less than 5 per cent by weight, but sufficient so that when the vegetable oil product is mixed with refined groundnut oil it is in the proportion of 20 : 80.[3]

The Government was so greatly upset over the public apprehension that in addition to the statutory step already taken, it set up in 1947 a committee called Ghee Adulteration

Committee. The Committee was to suggest other measures and ways to prevent adulteration of ghee with vanaspati.

The statutory provision of adding five per cent of sesame oil was not regarded as a foolproof[4] measure for preventing vanaspati from being used as an adulterant. The scientists were therefore, entrusted with the task of finding out a suitable colouring agent which could be added to vanaspati. The Government was determined to find colouring agent. Efforts went on in this direction in full gear.

The essential qualities of the colouring agent were :[5]

- —it should be inexpensive,
- —it should not be toxic,
- —it should be capable of being added in a small quantity— and should be detectable by simple tests by a housewife at home,
- —once the agent has been added to vanaspati it should be impossible to separate it by any means,
- —it should be helpful in detecting adulteration even if a small quantity, say five per cent of vanaspati is mixed with 'desi' ghee,
- —it should not adversely affect the quality of vanaspati when added to it,
- —it should not be injurious to health,
- —it should form a solution in vanaspati and should be such as could easily be incorporated,
- —it should not be repulsive in look, taste or smell.

Numerous colours and chemicals suggested by various committees set up to tackle this problem were experimented upon. None of them, however, was found suitable. The following chemical compounds were suggested:

First was colourless chemical compound 3, 5, 3^1, 5^1—tetra-butyl, 4, 4^1 dihydroxy-diphenyl methane suggested by the National Chemical Laboratory, Poona.

'Ratanjot' (Onosina echoides) root dye was another agent suggested for colouring vanaspati to prevent it from being used as an adulterant. The Drug Research Institute, Lucknow, examined it. It was found to be unsuitable for the purpose because the colour could be removed after giving the compound some chemical treatment.

In 1952, a material pink in colour was found out by the Government.[6]

This was also not found to be a suitable colour because the Government wanted yellow colour.

The Ghee Adulteration Committee adopted a resolution in 1952 through which the Government decided to defer the use of visible colouring material as an agent to colour vanaspati till the reports of various other experiments being carried on in this regard were available and had been studied by it.

In 1960, under great public pressure, the Government of India again appointed[7] a committee of experts to coordinate the research for finding out a suitable colouring material for vanaspati.

The expert committee considered all the researches being done in this regard and concluded that the choice for a colouring material for vanaspati was limited to the following :

ratanjot dye,
alcohol extract of turmeric,
copper chlorophyl, and
a synthetic yellow colour prepared from 4, 4′ dihydroxy, z, z[1], 6′ tetrabutyl diphenyl methane.

The expert committee examined in detail the possibility or otherwise of using any of the above dyes for use as an additive to vanaspati to prevent it from being used as an adulterant. None of them, however, was found to be suitable by the committee. Each one was found to be deficient in one respect or the other. Ratanjot root dye required further researches regarding its toxicity. Alcohol extract of turmeric was not found to be a perfect dye as further research was being carried on to make it mixable with vanaspati. Apart from the experiments being carried on in the laboratories, the Government had its own reservations about the use of alcoholic extracts of turmeric. The Government was of the view that this dye would, instead of preventing adulteration, in fact, promote it. Its colour when mixed with vanaspati in a light shade would give the mixture the appearance of 'cow ghee.'[8] Regarding copper cholorophyl it was apprehended that since the dye had a copper content it would surely be unfit for internal consumption. It had been established by scientists that copper in whatever form and howsoever little in quantity if taken internally is a health hazard. Hence, this dye required further researches before it could be recommended for use by the vanaspati industry. The last one—the synthetic yellow colour—also was required to be investigated further.

The expert committee therefore made the following recommendations regarding the colouring of vanaspati :[9]

(i) The colouring of vanaspati is neither practicable nor desirable.

(ii) Alternative method 'more rigorous enforcement' of manufacturing standards and marketing of ghee in small containers with Agmark. Agmark seals should be used for achieving the end in view.

(iii) The colouring of vanaspati with sesame oil currently in force which imparts a red tinge to vanaspati on subjecting it to a simple test called Baudouin Test should amply be sufficient.

Though the Government accepted the above recommendations of the Experts Committee, the controversy had not been buried finally. Every now and then the Members of Parliament asked questions in the House about the latest position on the finding of a colour dye for vanaspati. The Members were informed in 1971[10] and again as late as in 1977[11] that efforts were still being made to find a suitable medium to colour vanaspati. But so far it has not succeeded.

The official stand of the Government has always been that the search has not been given up. But the fact is that a suitable colour dye has not yet been found.

Taking the last recommendation of the Coordination Committee into account, there is no need at all to continue the search and the public should be finally told that there is no need for colouring vanaspati.

As regards adulteration of 'ghee' with vanaspati, the Government has to check adulteration of vanaspati itself. These days vanaspati has ceased to be an adulterant for 'desi' ghee. This is because vanaspati is always in short supply though it is cheaper than the 'desi' ghee.

There has been an unnecessary stress on adulteration of 'desi' ghee with vanaspati from the very beginning perhaps because vanaspati was used in the early days only for this purpose. Nowadays adulteration has become a fashion. According to the Lok Sabha[12] practically everything is adulterated, why then single out vanaspati ? The Government should strengthen its machinery to check adulteration rather than punish the industry.

It is, therefore, suggested that once and for all this controversy should be ended. Vanaspati industry should not face it like Democle's Sword.

REFERENCES

1. *Constituent Assembly of India Legislature Debates*, Part I, Question and Answer, Official Reports for 8th December 1949, Vol. 4, pp. 283-187.
2. Notification No. 2 VP (2)/47 dt. 9 August 1947.
3. ibid
4. G.S. Hattangadi, *The Vanaspati Industry*, Indian Council of Oil Seeds, Bombay, 1958, p. 56.
5. ibid.
6. Information given by the Government to the Estimates Committee (Second Lok Sabha), Lok Sabha Secretariat, New Delhi, Part IV, 1959-60, *National Laboratories & Miscellaneous*, p. 22.
7. Note submitted by the Government of India to the Estimates Committee of the Lok Sabha 1960.
8. Note submitted by the Government of India to the Estimates Committee of the Lok Sabha in March, 1960.
9. Lok Sabha Starred Question No. 604 asked on 22.8.1968, *Lok Sabha Debates* 4 Series, Vol. 20, 1980.
10. Lok Sabha Unstarred Question No. 1044 asked on 22.11.71, *Lok Sabha Debates*, Series 15, Vol. VIII.
11. Lok Sabha Unstarred Question No. 6296 asked on 5.8.1977, *Lok Sabha Debates* Series 60, Vol. VI.
12. P. S. Lokanathan. Consumes at Sea in Shri S. Neela Maghan (ed.) *Marketing Management and Indian Economy*, Vikas Publication, New Delhi, 1969, pp. 177-87.

10

Government and the Industry

GOVERNMENT policies towards the synthetic fats industry should have two main objectives in view. First, the industry, being an essential food industry, should be seen to produce in the most hygienic conditions, and secondly, being an essential industry, the Government policy towards the price of vanaspati should be such as not to mar the production nor leave the consumers at the mercy of the manufacturers and traders. Government policies assume great importance in the days of controversy between the industry and the Government.

Policies on Margarine Production

Vanaspati and margarine being newly introduced food articles, it was but natural that the general public should be apprehensive about their quality, etc. The Governments of Western countries therefore took upon themselves to enforce controls regarding the quality of their products.

Margarine was subjected to several restrictive legislations in the U.S.A. as well as in other countries. The Oleomargarine Act of 1886[1] was the earliest legislation. The U.S. Government imposed a prohibitive tax on yellow margarine, levied high licence fees on all manufacturers, wholesalers and retailers of the product and in all respects subjected the manufacture and sale of oleomargarine to numerous restrictions. The object was not only to prevent margarine from reaching its normal consumption level but also for quite some time to prevent sale of any yellow margarine. The reason was that it looked like butter. Thereafter, there was a wave of similar legislations in which all American States took part. The reason, was however, different. They thought that its manufacture was not in the national interest. Besides being akin to butter in appearance, margarine was manufactured out of coconut, palm and palm kernel oils which were imported and that retarded the production of cottonseed and soyabean oils in the American States. The opponents, however, changed their attitude after manufacturers of margarine started using soyabean and other vegetable oils. In 1923, margarine was statutorily fortified with Vitamin A and D. According to the American Law enforced in 1941 the standards prescribed for their ingredients to be used in the manufacture of margarine not only served as Government recognition of the wholesomeness of the product, but also ensured protection of the consumer against the health hazards. These days not only are there no restrictions on the manufacture of margarine in America but the manufacturers can even add colour and essence akin to that of butter.[2]

Nutritionally, the value of margarine has been proved to be good as of a food fat with primary source of food fuel and of other nutritional factors. From the very early period margarine in the U.S.A. was fortified with at least 15,000 U.S.P. units of Vitamin A.[3]

The Government controls industries under its various statutes. For example, the framework for licensing and regulating industrial investments in the country is provided in the Industries (Development and Regulation) Act, 1951. In accordance with this Act, the Government is empowered to (i) force all the undertakings mentioned in the Schedule of Industries to register with it, and (ii) no new industrial undertaking can be established or any substantial extension to existing plants carried out without licence from the Government. The price and distribution of essential commodities are controlled under the Essential Commodities Act, 1948.

Vanaspati industry is one of those industries which are registered in the Schedule of Industries. This industry is also subject to the controls under the Act of 1951. For establishing a new unit (or for expansion of the installed capacity) permission of the Government is necessary.

Control on Quality of Vanaspati

Prior to 1947, there was no Central law controlling the quality of vanaspati. Some of the then provinces had prescribed standards for vanaspati under their own Food Rules. But their laws were not enforced strictly. During World War II production of vanaspati had increased at a phenomenal rate, and a large proportion of the product was supplied to the defence personnel. During the post-war period there was considerable agitation in the country against the use of vanaspati. In order to control effectively the manufacturer, stock and sale of vanaspati, the Government of India promulgated, in 1947,[4] what is known as the Vegetable Oil Product Control Order, under the Essential Supplies (Temporary Powers) Act, 1946. Under this Order the specifications of vanaspati were fully prescribed. In these specifications maximum limit for the melting point of vanaspati was prescribed at 37°C. This was so because it is almost identical with the body's temperature at which product is easily digested and assimilated in the body. Another thing in the specification was the incorporation of Vitamin 'A' at the level of 700[5] International Units per ounce of vanaspati. It was made obligatory on the part of the manufacturers of vanaspati to follow the specification of the Order of 1947. This makes the product as rich in respect of Vitamin 'A' as cow ghee. Addition of sesame oil at the rate of five per cent[6] had also been made compulsory by the Government. It was added to make detection of adulteration of ghee with vanaspati easier. Thus the Order provided the specifications in a manner that silenced the critics of vanaspati during those days.

It has also been suggested, though it is optional, that Vitamin 'D' at the rate of 50 International Units per ounce of vanaspati should be added to it.[7] For enforcement of control on quality of vanaspati four Inspectors have been posted at each of the four Zones at Delhi, Bombay, Calcutta, and Madras. They visit the factories in their respective zones and collect samples of vanaspati being manufactured in these factories. The samples are analysed in the Vanaspati Laboratory at Delhi. If the sample is found to be containing an adulterant material or not conforming to the specifications mentioned in the control order of 1947 action is taken against the manufacturer. The Inspectors also keep a watch on the hygienic conditions of the factories as also personally verify the records relating to Vitamin 'A', sesame oil, Baudouin test from the registers, etc., as a further check on the quality of the product. Mostly the factories maintain the quality.[8] Only very rarely the samples fail to conform to the specifications. Even these rare failures are taken up by the Government. The Government warns or even prosecutes the factories whose samples fall short of the prescribed specifications. On the recommendations[9] of the Estimates Committee of the Lok Sabha, the Government has sought the assistance of the Vanaspati Manufacturers Association of India to impress upon the manufacturers that they should not contravene the prescribed specification of vanaspati.[10]

Price Control

The pattern of price control on vanaspati has almost classical in its regularity. There were no controls between 1930 and 1943. The first price control was imposed by the Government during the Second World War. The purpose of this control was to ensure that the demand of the armed forces, which had increased to 25 per cent, was met. Another purpose was to regulate the price of vanaspati. This control continued up to 1952. The era of 1952-1963 was without any price control. The Government re-imposed the price control in February, 1963. The then Finance Minister, Shri Morarji Desai, imposed it by freezing the price level prevailing on 1 February, 1963. This was done to check vanaspati manufacturers from raising the prices of vanaspati, consequent upon abolition of excise duty (Rs. 110 per tonne) on vegetable oils but raising of it on vanaspati from Rs. 200 to Rs. 320 per tonne. The industry was assured by the Gevernment that the price freeze was temporary. The behaviour of prices of vegetable oils after abolition of excise duty was contrary to the expectations of the Government. They rose and the industry found it uneconomic to produce vanaspati and sell it at the price level of 1 February, 1963. The price freeze was, therefore, replaced by official price control from 21 May, 1963. The price formula followed by the Government from 21 May, 1963, was revised on the basis of an inquiry conducted into the cost structure of vanaspati. The industry was also helpless but had no option but to follow the Government policy, although because of erratic behaviour of prices of vegetable oils due to low oilseed production, the price controls had ceased to have any meaning. The industry requested the Government several times but in vain to lift the price control on vanaspati. A strong plea was made by the industry in May, 1968, for lifting the price controls. It was also not heeded although vegetable oil was easily available in sufficient quantity in the country.

In 1966, on devaluation of the rupee, the government decided to import vegetable oil from the U.S.A. and the U.S.S.R. and supply it to manufacturers of vanaspati to supplement the indigenous oil supply. The idea of the government to bring stability in the oil prices with the import of oil did not, however, materialise. The arrival of imported oil was erratic and irregular. The very purpose for which imports of oil had been resorted to was defeated. The prices of indigenous oil continued to be fluctuating. The erratic and irregular import of oils from abroad did not prompt the Government to abolish or to even suspend price controls. On the contrary a very funny formula was devised by the Government. It was named as 'Notional Use'[11] of imported oil. Under this formula the use of imported oil was presumed even when the imported oil was not made available to the industry. The price of vanaspati was fixed on the assumption of use of imported oil. It was a fantastic formula. Perhaps vanaspati is the only industry wherein the price of a finished produce was fixed and regulated on the basis of a raw material which was never made available to the industry.

At last the Government agreed to[12] lifting of price controls but to safeguard the consumer's interest it wanted an assurance from industry that it would follow the existing pattern of processing and costs and any increase or decrease in the vanaspati prices would be solely with relation to fluctuations in the vegetable oil prices. The industry, rightly, did not agree and hence the controls were not lifted.

On 5 September, 1968, despite the disapproval of the Government the vanaspati Manufacturers Association unilaterally increased the prices of Vanaspati in different zones in utter disregard of the then existing voluntary control. As the reasons given by the manufacturers were not found convincing by the Government, it retaliated by imposing statutory controls on the prices of vanaspati with effect from 6

September, 1968.[13] Under the statutory controls, the Government started fixing prices of vanaspati on zonal basis. The disagreement between the industry and the Government made the situation acute. As a result the government took over distribution of vanaspati, and continued fixing prices of vanaspati on the basis of the zonal formula. It was also controlling the prices of the imported soyabean and sunflower oils received either as gift or at very cheap rates which they supplied to the industry.

In 1969, the Government asked the Tariff Commission to determine the production costs of vanaspati to enable it to decide about the continuance or otherwise of the statutory price controls on vanaspati.

The Tariff Commission studied the problems of this industry and recommended consideration of the following elements while fixing prices of vanaspati :

— a zonal oil base respresenting the weighted average purchase price of the previous fortnight including the price of imported oil, if any,
— conversion costs established for the zone on the basis of a simple study, and
— uniform rate of return at 12 per cent.

These recommendations were accepted by the Goverment.

During the period 1969-1974 the statutory price controls remained despite fluctuaticn in the price of indigenous oils and erratic and irregular supply of imported oils. To ease the situation the Government imposed restrictions in the use of oil for manufacture of vanaspati. Maximum limit for use of groundnut oil was fixed at 25 per cent and the use of non-traditional oils was allowed for manufacture of vanaspati. The State Trading Corporation, however, failed to keep up the supply of imported oil. The natural result was pressure on the indigenous oils and rise in the price of these oils.

The government also started holding back the fortnightly review of prices, sometimes even for three months. These measures were severely criticized by the industry as well as by the public. In spite of all the criticism, the price controls continued till the development of a crisis in the industry in 1974. The production came down to just half the requirements of the country, the main reason being stoppages, after May, 1974, by the Government of supply of imported oil at subsidised rates to the manufacturers. The result was that the industry was forced to cut down production to minimize its losses. The greatest absurdity was that during those days of price controls the Government wanted the industry to sell vanaspati at a price (after processing) which was even lower than the market price of the raw oil. But there was no control on the prices of vegetable oils—the basic raw material—used in the manufacture of vanaspati. And the Government was continuing with the price control on the finished product. However, in December 1974, the Government issued an order decontrolling vanaspati from 1 January, 1975.

Effects of Price Control

There can be no two opinions that the measures of imposing statutory controls on the prices of vanaspati were taken by the Government keeping the interests of the consumer in view. It thought that the industry was exploiting the consumer. Yet, if examined closely, it would be seen that the consumer never benefited from those measures. He continued to pay high price for vanaspati. On the other hand, had the Government left the industry alone to produce vanaspati and supply it to the consumer at competitive rates, he would have definitely benefited. The only thing that the Government had to ensure was that industry got continuous supply of raw vegetable oils. At least during 1966-67 the Government could have lifted the controls or suspended them when the groundnut oil was available in a fairly good quantity in the country and the Government had also imported 3 lakh tonnes of fats and oils from the U.S.A. and the U.S.S.R. Despite all these favourable circumstances the consumer had continued to pay the same prices for vanaspati. The industry began reducing production of vanaspati. They knew that if it continued to produce vanaspati in the same quantity as before it would be losing. The recession had set in the vanaspati industry as well. Since then there has been an increase in the prices of groundnut oil in the country and the industry's plea for lifting of the price control did not find favour with the government. The Government tried to keep the prices of vanaspati down despite rising prices of groundnut oil in the country. The industry pleaded for a rise in the prices of vanaspati after every spurt in the prices of groundnut oil. The argument of the industry was that if the Government wanted that there should be stability in the prices of vanaspati, the prices of edible oils should be controlled. This was impossible because edible oils, in substantial quantities were and still are being produced in the unorganized sector spread all over the countryside.[14]

The Government could try but apprehended that removal of price controls on vanaspati would bring about a sudden rise in the price of vanaspati and hit the consumer very hard. But this argument could be met by the fact that vanaspati was not a cereal for which there is no substitute. Consumers, whenever finding vanaspati too expensive, generally easily switched over to unrefined oils or cut down their consumption or did both. Thus on the basis of the simple formula in economics that the demand of vanaspati is elastic because it has substitutes, its prices could affect its consumption to a great extent. The substitutes of vanaspati could act as a built-in check against moderate increases in the prices of vanaspati as in the case with the commodities with elastic demand. It is also an open secret now that there was price competition within the industry. It was found that whenever the supply position of vegetable oils eased the vanaspati manufacturers sold vanaspati at prices lower than those fixed statutorily by the Government.

The justification given by the Government for price control was that vanaspati industry was being supplied cheaper oil, as such the benefit of lower priced oil should go to the consumers and not to the industry. In practice it was not so. The industry was not benefited at all on the ground of supply of cheaper soyabean oil on account of the following reasons :

(i) Soyabean oil processing costs are higher and also it takes longer to refine it and it results in lesser and costlier production.

(ii) There was no clearcut policy of the Government whereby the industry could anticipate the extent to which soyabean oil use would be permitted, and it could plan procurement of oils for maintaining vanaspati production rationally. If suddenly the percentage of soyabean oil used was reduced substantially there might not have been enough other oil in the stock of factories to maintain production. On the other hand, if the use of soyabean oil was raised factories having bought indigenous oils assuming lower soyabean oil usage were faced with the problems of finance and storage.

(iii) The prices of soyabean oil were varied by the Government. In fact the Government had been getting it at dock price from the U.S.A. under PL 480 although now it has to purchase it in the open market. Even then it was cheaper than the indigenous groundnut oil.[15] It should be sold to the industry without any profit whatsoever. But the Government would not do this. Here is an illustration :

The import prices of soyabean oil inclusive of customs duty and incidental charges during January-May and August-September, 1968, were Rs. 2,525 and Rs. 2,139 per tonne respectively. The prices fixed by the Government during the period July-October 1968, were as under.[16]

Period	Price (per tonne)
9 July to 26 July 1968	Rs. 2025 to Rs. 2460
27 July to 8 August 1968	Rs. 2145 to Rs. 2635
9 August to 31 October 1968	Rs. 2550 to Rs. 2850

The explanation of the Government[17] that the prices of soyabean were fixed in such a manner as might not allow any rise in the prices of groundnut oil was not convincing at all.

Thus the conclusion that the controls on vanaspati prices did not help to mitigate the sufferings of the consumers on account of fluctuations in the indigenous oil prices is correct. It did not also help the consumer to get full benefit of the cheaper imported oils. The price control, on the other hand, upset the vanaspati oil price parities, distorted production and created artificial shortages. With large surplus production capacity competition would have ensured that consumers got their supplies of vanaspati at reasonable prices and this would have also made the price control unnecessary even for regulating margins of the vanaspati manufacturers if there are no price controls. Therefore, this should be lifted. In addition, there was large surplus capacity of industry. It could have surely ensured reasonable prices through competition.

Effect of Decontrol

After decontrol there was marked improvement in the supply position of vanaspati. The industry's consumption of vegetable oil rose to 5.3 lakh tonnes in 1975 from a meagre 3.4 lakh tonnes in 1974. This shows the extent to which vanaspati production rose in 1975. The production of vanaspati also rose from 3.53 lakh tonnes in 1974-75 to 5 lakh tonnes in 1975-76. Since then it has continued to rise and it is also since then that the country has never faced shortage of vanaspati. There was a fall in the prices of vanaspati immediately on decontrol. During the year 1974-75 the wholesale price index had gone up to 172.4. It fell to 134.9 in 1975-76[18] immediately after decontrol. There is another aspect of decontrol of vanaspati. It has affected the industry adversely in the Eastern Sector. In this sector production of oilseeds is almost nil. The entire requirements of raw vegetable oil, the main raw material for vanaspati manufacture, has to be imported from surplus States of Gujarat, A.P., Maharashtra, etc.

With the delicensing of industry many units were set up in the oil producing States with the result that other States considerably reduced the supply of vegetable oils to vanaspati manufacturers in the Eastern Sector. This shortage of raw materials was, however, made up by supply of subsidised imported oil to the manufacturers in that sector. The decontrol of vanaspati put every unit of vanaspati situated in the East Zone at a distinct disadvantage. The units in the oil-producing States produce oil and vanaspati and refine oil at cheaper rates and then transport it to the Eastern Zone at a price which renders production of vanaspati in that zone very costly. This has resulted in reduction in the utilization of installed capacity of the industry up to 10 per cent.[19] For an economic production a unit must use at least 50 per cent of its installed capacity. Even shifting to refining the vegetable oils in the Eastern Zone will not be helpful as the basic disadvantage of the additional cost of transport of oil from the surplus States would still be there.

Another effect of decontrol of vanaspati was that the price of vanaspati, the finished product, has fluctuated in sympathy with that of vegetable oil. During May, 1977, vanaspati was selling at Rs 99.65 for 16.50 kg. when the cost of groundnut oil was Rs. 4,500 per tonne and that of sesame oil Rs. 5,600 per tonne. In April, 1977, the cost of a tonne of groundnut oil was Rs. 9,100 and that of sesame oil was Rs. 9,300. Vanaspati prices also rose to Rs. 147 per 16.50 kg. The maximum price of vanaspati was Rs. 151.45 in June, 1971. But there was a corresponding increase in the wholesale prices of groundnut and sesame oils (Rs. 9,700 and 8,700 per tonne respectively). The price of these two oils fell in October, 1977 to Rs.6 ,400 and Rs. 7,300 respectively. There was a corresponding fall in the wholesale prices of vanaspati which fell to Rs. 146 per 16.50 kg. At present there is no[20] statutory control on the production, distribution and pricing of vanaspati. The industry has agreed to voluntary discipline in pricing and distribution of vanaspati. There is no change as yet in this position.

Present Position

Still it cannot be said that vanaspati industry is without any Government control. Although there is no statutory price control, whenever there is any abnormal rise in the prices of vanaspati, the Government consults the manufacturers and tries to bring the prices down.

At present the industry is using 90 per cent of imported oil for manufacture of vanaspati. For this purpose the Government does not even hesitate to issue licence to private consumers to import oil directly and ease the pressure on the indigenous oil resources. The industry depends these days fully on the Government for supply of this most important raw material, for its requirement of palm oil which the industry is at present using for manufacture of vanaspati. Seventy-five per cent of the industry's requirements of palm oil and other vagetable oils is met by the State Trading Corporation through imports. Thus, indirect control of the Government on the industry is still there. But it can be said that the Government's attitude to the industry is helpful. In cases of any complaints that the supply of imported oil does not reach them in time, the Government has tried to help by allowing the private trades to import edible oil under the Open General Licence.

During 1976-77, import licences worth Rs. 625 crores[21] were issued. The trader community, did not fully use this facility offered by the Government. Actual imports of oils against the abovementioned licences were only worth Rs. 50 crores[22] though by September, 1977, another Rs. 70 crores[23] worth of oil was received.

In fact the traders instead of importing oil procured against their licences into India had sold it in the international market as it found it more profitable. This greatly annoyed the Government. Hereafter, therfore, the Government became wiser and took adequate precautions to prevent any misuse of import licences issued to traders. At present most of the vegetable edible oil is imported through the STC although the import licences to private parties are also issued. But these are subject to conditions laid down for use of such licences within a specified period. Thus there are minimal chances of misusing these licences.

The Government has been meeting the edible oil requirements of the vanaspati industry to the extent of 90 per cent[24] through imported oils and at present the usage of groundnut oil has virtually been prohibited.[25] To meet the shortage of vegetable oil and help the industry the quantum of import of edible oils has been increased eightfold, in three years' time. During 1975, 55,505 tonnes of edible oil was imported which rose to 1,23,503 tonnes in 1976 and to 4,97,876 tonnes in 1977.[26]

According to the information given[27] to Parliament by the Government in 1977 the industry was fully dependent on imported oil distributed through the STC.

Although the price control has been completely lifted it cannot be said that the vanaspati industry is totally free from any control from the Government. Not only the Government has still full authority to check the quality of vanaspati produced, it also exercise control on the use of vegetable oil. For example, (i) every factory having a capacity of more than 50 tonnes a day has to inform the Government telegraphically about its production on the previous day, (ii) every week every factory has to submit a return of production to the Government, and (iii) the return which the factory has to send to the Government every week must contain the details of different oils used by the factory for manufacture of vanaspati.[28]

REFERENCES

1. *Encyclopaedia Britannica*, Vol. 14, p. 864.
2. *Encyclopaedia Americana* (American Corporation), Vol. 18, p. 229.
3. ibid.
4. Office Memorandum No. 2VP(2) 47 dated 9 August, 1947, Dept. of Food, Government of India.
5. Notification No. S.R.O.V. 80 dated 21 October, 1950, Dept. of Food, Government of India.
6. ibid.
7. Letter No. 5-VP(4)/51 dated 3 April, 1961, from the Vegetable Product Controller of India to all Vegetable Oil Product Factories.
8. *Lok Sabha Debates*, 4th Series, Vol. 20, 1968, Cols. 18, 19, Lok Sabha Secretariat, New Delhi, 1968.
9. *Estimates Committee 1960-61* (Second Lok Sabha, India), Lok Sabha Secretariate, New Delhi, 1960 Report No. 127, p. 30, Paras 58-59.
10. Ministry of Food and Agriculture (Department of Food). Office Memorandum No. 9-1/6 15 Adm. dated 17 October, 1961.
11. A Study of Price Controls on the Industry NCAER.
12. *Lok Sabha Debates*, 5th Series, Vol. 17, 1968, Lok Sabha Unstarred Question asked on 9 May, 1968, Col. 3074.
13. *Lok Sabha Debates*, 4th Series, Vol. 21, 1968, Lok Sabha Starred Question No. 110 asked on 14 November, 1968 Col. 44.
14. *Lok Sabha Debates*, 4th Series, Vol. 32, 1970, Col. 103.
15. Speech of George Fernandes, ex-M.P. in the Lok Sabha on 28 November, 1968, *Hindustan Times*, 29 November, 1968.
16. Lok Sabha Unstarred Question asked on 28 November, 1968, *Lok Sabha Debates*, 4th Series, Vol. 22 Col. 9.
17. Speech of Shri Jagjivan Ram, former Food Minister, in the Lok Sabha on 28 November, 1968, *Hindustan Times*, 29, November, 1968.
18. Lok Sabha Unstarred Question No. 10192 answered on 12 May, 1978, *Lok Sabha Debate*, 6th Series, Vol. XV.
19. 'Vanaspati Industry in Eastern Sector' by V. N. Tantia, *Eastern Economist*, 6 August, 1977, pp. 294-195.
20 Lok Sabha Starred Question No. 487 answered on 15 July, 1977, *Lok Sabha Debates*, 6th Series, Vol. IV. Col. 42 and 43.
21. Short-notice Question No. 9 answered in the Lok Sabha on July, 1977, *Lok Sabha Debates*, 6th Series.
22. ibid.
23. ibid.
24. Unstarred Question No. 872 answered on 17 June, 1977.
25. Unstarred Question No. 57 answered on 19 June, 1977.
26. Unstarred Question No. 1272 answered on 20 February, 1977 (compiled from information given to Parliament).
27. Unstarred Question No. 2337 answered on 1 July, 1977.
28. Letter of A.C. Challapathi, published in the *Economic Political Weekly* dt.3.8.74, 1273.

11

Problems and Conclusions

VANASPATI INDUSTRY is one of the biggest food processing industries ranking next to sugar in India. Sugar industry is fortunate to have the support of the consumer because he cannot do without it. But the vanaspati industry has been the subject of a lot of public criticism. This is because of inadequate supply and ever fluctuating prices. The greatest irony is that even though the installed capacity is much more than the demand, vanaspati sometimes disappears from the market to the great harassment of the consumer.

The industry is faced with the shortage and high cost of edible oils, shortage and high costs of packing materials. There are scores of taxes and the confusing policy of the Government. These are the ills which the industry has been suffering from.

Shortage of Edible Oil

Shortage of edible oil which is the basic raw material for manufacturing vanaspati has hit the industry very hard. Since the very beginning this industry has been faced with this problem. Even today there is no improvement in the position of indigenous oil supply. To ease the situation the Government started import of edible vegetable oils—soyabean oil from the U.S.A and sunflower oil from the U.S.S.R. Table 11.1 shows the import of oils.

During the oil year 1976-77 the demand for oil was 32 lakh tonnes and the supply was only 24 lakh tonnes. The deficit of 8 lakh tonnes was made up by importing oil from abroad.[1]

After 1975, the year in which the statutory price control

TABLE 11.1

Import of Vegetable Oil during 1965-75

Year	Quantity (in tonnes)
1965	58000
1969	112534
1973	106748
1974	81447
1975	51136

was lifted by the Government, the import of edible oils was made in sufficient quantities. The entire shortage of oil was met. During 1977-78 the total demand for oil including the oil required for manufacture of vanaspati in the country was 33.42 lakh tonnes. The total supply from the indigenous sources was only 26.78 lakh tonnes.[2] The shortage of 6.64 lakh tonnes was made up by importing edible oils from abroad.

In fact the Government had proposed to import 9.5 lakh tonnes[3] of edible oil during the oil year 1977-78. Similarly during 1978-79 against a total demand of 35.91 lakh tonnes[4] of edible oils the country's production was only 28.08 lakh tonnes. The entire deficit of 7.83 lakh tonnes was met through imports.

The greatest tragedy is that in spite of import of vegetable oils costing Rs. 600 crores in foreign exchange the common man is still finding it impossible to bring it to his kicthen.

At present there is a stagnation in the growth rate of oilseed production. The reasons are not for to seek. The most important ones are :

— neglect of oilseed crops by States and the Centre,

— concentration of research on food production, oilseeds were neglected.

— hardly five per cent of the area where oilseeds are grown has irrigation facilities. Mostly the cultivation of oilseeds depends on weather gods.

—on account of uncertainty of rains the farmers consider any investment in fertilizers, improved seeds, plant protection measures, etc., too risky to be undertaken. Therefore the production of oilseed passes through a vicious circle.

Who is responsible for such a situation? There are two factors—human and natural. On the human side wrong policies of export/import, inter-state movement and of distribution are responsible. On the natural, failure of the monsoon for the past two years. Together they are responsible for the acute shortage of oilseeds and vegetable oils in India. However, imports have saved situation but only for a temporary period. The industry needs a permanent cure for its ills and not palliatives.

An analysis of the root cause of shortage of edible oils in the country shows that it is linked with the shortage in the production of oilseeds in the country. For eradicating this cause, in the first instance, the causes of low production of oilseeds will have to be highlighted. These can be enumerated as under:

Low Productivity

Table 11.2 shows yield per acre of groundnut and sesame oilseeds:

TABLE 11.2[5]

Per-acre yield of Groundnut and Sesame in India and Some other Countries of the World

Name of the Country	Yield per acre in kgs. for a triennium	
	Groundnut	Sesame
India	298	72
China	365	148
U S.A.	598	—
Nigeria	655	—
Brazil	523	—
Pakistan	—	163
Mexico	—	268
Turkey	—	225
Others	226	300

It will be seen from Table 11.2 that this yield per acre in India compared to the countries shown is the lowest in respect of both the oilseeds. The worst part is that the growth rate of output and yield has been increasingly poor. In 1964-65 it was 1.8 per cent and in 1976-77 it still went down. Futher even the acreage under groundnut fell during the six-year period. It was 7.326 million hectares in 1970. It came down to 7.043 million hectares in 1976-77. There was, however, some improvement in 1977-78 when the total area under groundnut cultivation in the country rose to 7.175 million hectares.[6]

Another fact which is beyond comprehension is that since 1930 the acreage under cultivation of groundnut has been increasing, the yield per acre is declining. This can be seen from the following figures:

Year	*Land under cultivation under groundnut*[7]
1930	1.6187 million hectares
1952	7.7516 ,, ,,
1966-67	7.2844 ,, ,,
1976-77	7.043 ,, ,,
1977-78	7.175 ,, ,,

This is a dismal situation. The land in India can certainly be made to yield much more than what it is producing at present. The Government was aware of it as early as in 1954. But nothing concrete seems to have been done to increase the yield per acre of groundnut crop in India.

During the First Five-year Plan period no special efforts were made for raising oilseed production. Whatever increase was there it was natural. During the Second Plan period, for the first two years no effort was made, but in the middle of the Plan period the Government woke up to the need for augmenting oilseed production in the country.

The State governments were asked to formulate integrated oilseed development plans with joint finances from the Centre and State exchequers. By the time the schemes were drawn up and staff provided the Plan period ended and virtually nothing was done. During the Third Plan period the Central Government sponsored some package programmes and provided special funds. But again the State Governments did not take enough interest. As such not much headway could be made. The Centre, of course, took up some special programmes for increasing groundnut production by providing funds for oilseed development and appointing special staff for intensive extension works. It covered 32 lakh acres of groundnut area. But the most surprising thing is that the Governments of Gujarat and Maharasthra States, the home of groundnut production, were cool towards the Centre's package programmes because they were asked to share the cast of the development schemes. So not much could be achieved and the package programmes did not make much headway.

Another instance of such attitude towards the growth of oilseeds in India is the typical indifference to variety No. TMV-2—an improved variety of groundnut—introduced 40 years ago in the southern States. This has not been further improved or developed.[8]

Efforts of VMA

The Vanaspati Manufacturers' Association has done a yeoman's service for the groundnut growers and indirectly for the industry. Knowing the unhelpful attitude of the Central as well as State Governments towards the development of groundnut production in India, it made its first humble effort in two selected villages, Jalia and Shindi in Saurashtra and Khandesh respectively, in 1962 at a cost of Rs. 10,000.[9]

It continued to contribute its mite and spent Rs. 1,60,000 in 1965 and Rs. 3,90,309 in 1969[10] on the same project. Gradually its programmes covered the States of Punjab, Rajasthan, Mysore and more areas of Gujarat and Maharashtra. The Association also demonstrated that the Hissar area in Haryana and Rajasthan canal areas could raise bumper groundnut harvests with the help of two or three irrigations.

The Association's project with its high yield achievement became so popular that soon the State Governments began to seek its help for popularizing improved methods of cultivation of groundnut among the cultivators.[11] And the Association has fully associated itself with the efforts of the State Governments and has extended its activities towards (i) popularizing improved varieties of groundnut seeds among the cultivators; (ii) extending the area under groundnut for the cultivation of new potential areas; (iii) extending technical guidance, and (iv) training State extension staff. The Association's efforts have yielded good results. It has now extended its programme to 14 States covering 4,000 villages and 28,000 hectares of groundnut cultivations. There was a 40 per cent increase in the yield because of the above efforts of the Association. It has also taken up large-scale multiplication of improved varieties of groundnut developed by BARC and Agricultural Universities.[12]

Finding it difficult to meet the cost of its extension programme the Association requested for a levy of oil cess at the rate of Rs. 5 per tonne to meet this expenditure. It has not been acceded to so far by the Government.

It is suggested that the Government of India reconsider this favourably the request of the Association for the cess especially when it has been doing such useful work for increasing the groundnut oil supply in the country.

Diseases of Oilseeds

Indian oilseeds are severely damaged by several diseases, namely, blight, leaf-spot fungi, becteria and virus. Besides these there are several other diseases which can harm the oilseeds to some extent.

Although every disease requires separate and special treatment yet the following protective measures if undertaken by the farmers, can, to a great extent, either prevent the occurrence of the disease or, can nip them in the bud: (i) Treatment of seed with agrosn, (ii) Burning of affected plants (iii) Spraying of insecticides and pesticides.

Reduction in Cultivation Cost

Steps should be taken to reduce the cultivation cost of oilseeds in the country which will result in supply of cheaper vegetable oils required for vanaspati industry.

The need for such reduction has not been realized by the farmers. If the farmers could be educated on this and helped to reduce the cultivation costs by reducing expenditure on seeds, sowing, inter-cultivation and harvesting, appreciable savings could be affected. It is possible to reduce costs on these items because in most of the States labour-saving devices are not being used by the farmers. Old and orthodox agricultural implements could be advantageously replaced with the modern ones or improved upon. Power-driven implements could be used for cultivation. Preparatory cultivation and better manuring are some of the best ways to reduce the cost. The following could be used profitably by the farmers :

New Method of Sowing : It has been proved that sowing with seed drills helps to regulate seed rate and cover larger areas in a shorter time. The drills cover three to five acres in a day but require considerable skill and experience to operate them. The bullock-driven drill is more useful which is an improvement over the hand drills. The sowing can be done to any desired spacing by adjusting the tier and the seed plate. Such drilling reduces the sowing cost by nearly 50 per cent. Mechanical drills having double length of the bullock drills and with the feeding hoppers designed for use with trailers can cover 12 to 15 acres per day. This will result in saving of more land per-day and also in saving in over-all cost of oilseed sowing.

Preparatory Cultivation : The preparatory cultivation of fields before sowing provides a good seed bed, controls the weeds and utilizes the rainfall to the best advantage of the crop. Without a well-prepared seed bed, the germination is adversely affected and results in poor crop. Its further development is also observed to suffer a great deal in fields where the tilth is inadequate. All researchers and extension agronomists unanimously agree that the land should be thoroughly and completely prepared before cultivation. This results in minimizing the losses in seeds sown.

Manure : Oilseeds are considered to be great consumers of potash and lime. Thus if its several crops are grown without fertilizers subsequent crops may have acute deficiency of potash and nitrogen.

In India the common manure used for oilseeds is made up of dung, village sweepings, compost and ash. Its quantity depends upon numerous factors, viz. availability of manure, cost, distance of fields from the village, condition of crop, etc. But the normal quantity is 5-10 cartloads per acre.

Since dung is not available in sufficient quantity for oilseed cultivation, farmers have to depend on chemical fertilizers, e.g. ammonium sulphate, mono-ammonia sulphate, Dye urea, etc. Researches conducted in Tamil Nadu and Punjab have shown that the crop response to the application of 25 lbs. of nitrogen and ammonium sulphate is good. For instance, for a plentiful groundnut[13] crop the following quantities of fertilizers per hectare may be used in two different conditions as is usually done at the time of sowing. The results would be fine.

Rain-fed Areas		*Under-irrigated Areas*	
Nitrogen	30 kgs.	Nitrogen	40 kgs.
Phosphate	1 kg.	Phosphate	80 kgs.
Potash	20 kgs.	Potash	40 kgs.

Irrigation

Oilseeds, especially groundnuts, are grown mostly in areas where rainfall is scanty and irrigation facilities are inadequate. For example, Tamil Nadu, Andhra Pradesh and Gujarat. Here farmers have to depend mainly on wells and tanks which can irrigate only a limited area. These too are mostly utilized for irrigating foodgrain crops like wheat, rice, etc. Oilseeds are given second preference. Proper irrigation is necessary for the entire period of oilseed crop.

But the most important is the flowering period. It is at this time that there should be adequate water. Otherwise the flower will dry up. Prevention of this possible only when there are adequate irrigation facilities. With proper watering of the fields at flowering time there would be no shedding of buds and flowers and pods would be better and bigger.

As construction of canals will take a very long time it is suggested that the State and Central Governments should augment irrigation facilities by sinking tube-wells.

For a long-term plan when the giant national grid of irrigation system is executed it would revolutionize the irrigation facilities in the now drought-ridden areas of Tamil Nadu, Andhra Pradesh, Mysore and Gujarat.

Table 11.3 gives the State-wise irrigated areas under groundnut in 1968-69. There is not much improvement in this position even after more than a decade.

Good Quality Seeds : Good quality seeds should be used. It is suggested that : (i) In the case of 'groundnuts' 'Asiriya Mwitunde'[14], a Tanganyika variety with many desirable qualities, e.g. high resistance to disease and pests. Good response to irrigation and fertilization, introduced at the Regional Centre, Hyderabad, through Indian Agricultural

TABLE 11.3[15]

Statewise Irrigated Area under Groundnut

Irrigated Area (in Lakh hectares)

Region	Groundnut Area
Andhra Pradesh	1.54
Gujarat	0.12
Madhya Pradesh	0.01
Maharashtra	0.26
Punjab	0.19
Rajasthan	0.06
Tamil Nadu	1.40
U.P.	0.02
West Bengal	—
Union Territories	0.04
Total	3.64

Research Institute, New Delhi, has given encouraging results. The National Seed Corporation has also been distributing this particular variety in different States since 1966-67; (ii) for Sesame[16] 'Early Russian Variety' has the genesis of resistance to the bacterial diseases, 'Soudomonas Sesame' of 75-A/1-12 and NP-6 are tolerant to the disease 'Phytophthera'; ST-58 and Gwalior 5 is tolerant to Macrophomina Phaseoh. The variety 'Sirogama' and species radiatum are resistant to the disease 'Fusarium Oxysporium'.

Fair Prices to Oilseed Growers

With the increasing use of agricultural inputs the production of oilseeds would surely increase. There may even be a massive oilseed production. The Government should therefore reassure the farmer that he would get his price and would not be forced to make any stress sale. The Government is alive to this problem and has already fixed support prices for groundnuts and soyabean. In fact, NAFED, which is entrusted with the purchase of oilseeds at support prices, bought during 1976-77, 470 tonnes of soyabean. No purchase, however, was made of groundnut, sunflower and mustard because the market prices were higher than the support prices. The support prices fixed for various oilseeds were :

Item	*Support Price (in rupees)*
Groundnut	140 per quintal
Soyabean	145 ,,
Sunflower	150 ,,

During 1977-78 higher support prices were fixed. These are :

Item	*Support Price (in rupees)*
Groundnut	160 per quintal
Soyabean	145 ,,

During 1978-79 also the following support prices were fixed :[17]

Item	*Support Price (in rupees)*
Groundnut	175 per quintal
Soyabean	175 ,,
Sunflower	175 ,,

The support prices during 1978-79, as is clear, were the highest. There was another feature of the fixation of support prices for oilseeds. The sunflower was included in the list of oilseeds for which support prices were fixed by the Government to help the growers.

If the prices fell below the support price the NAFED was authorized to purchase these commodities at the abovementioned prices. Since the Government started fixing support prices for various oilseeds the growers have taken a sigh of relief. They are now not faced with distress sales of oilseeds to unscrupulous traders.

Storage of Oilseeds

Generally, farmers, intermediate and even mill-owners, store oilseeds in loose or in gunny bags. Besides, in godowns seeds are kept in the open spaces because there is no covered space. Where the rainfall is not heavy this method of storage in the open is possible. But where rains are heavy or even where there are threatening clouds in the sky these seeds are covered with tarpaulin or 'gunny purdah'. The farmers store them in their houses which are generally mud houses. They also do not afford the facility of spraying protective powder to save the seeds from being spoilt by insects or eaten up by rats. Thus, a huge quantity of oilseeds-groundnuts is wasted.

It is therefore, suggested that groundnuts should be stored as pods rather than as kernels. If it is necessary to store groundnuts as kernels for long periods, these should be dried so that the moisture content is reduced to below minimum five per cent. These should be decorticated so that the percentage of 'splits' and broken nuts is the minimum. Of the two crops of groundnut, the kernels from the winter (rain-fed) crops of should be stored for long periods and those from the summer crop should be crushed as early as possible. Kernels should be stored in well-ventilated godowns and the bags should be stacked on soft beds for example, of saw, but not more than 10 units high.

Groundnut oil or, for that matter, any other edible oil should preferably be stored in glass containers.[18] By storing it in metallic containers the quality deteriorates.[19]

Another precaution to keep the quality intact which should be taken in storing vegetable oil is that it should be stored at a place where neither light nor air can affect it.

The State Trading Corporation has no storage facility in North India to meet the requirements of the North Zone factories which account for nearly 45 per cent of vanaspati production in the country. Since availability of tank wagons for the movement of vegetable oil from Bombay, Calcutta and Kandla is not always assured, the factories are forced to work on notional usage of soyabean oil. When the use of soyabean oil is reduced for some period the S.T.C. with an idea to keep the regular flow of oil suddenly starts supplying huge quantities of oil to the manufacturers, creating storage difficulties and finance problems. If the S.T.C. arranges for a large storage tank at Delhi these difficulties can be obviated.

Promotion of Production of Soyabean

Encouraged by the possibility of utilizing soyabean oil for manufacture of vanaspati in India the Government took steps to popularize its cultivation in the country. It is being cultivated in various parts of the country, viz. from Kashmir to Nagaland in the northern hill region, and it was estimated that in 1958 the total area under soyabean cultivation was 43,000 acres.[20] The Government imported soyabean seeds from the U.S.A. and developed them in the I.A.R.I., Delhi, to suit Indian conditions. These can now be grown in Maharashtra, Gujarat, Mysore, Andhra Pradesh, Madhya Pradesh, etc.

In the beginning apprehensions were expressed about the difficulty of extracting oil from soyabean as there were not many solvent extraction plants. But as has been stated[21] by the Government the existing 71 units for cottonseed oil extraction can, with a slight adjustment in the machines and plants, be used for extracting oil from soyabean.

The Government has even fixed the procurement price of soyabean. The Food Corporation of India has been asked[22] to purchase at the rate of Rs. 85 a quintal any quantity of soyabean produced in the country.

This is really a good step forward for this new oilseed. It would encourage the cultivators to grow soyabean in the country because they are now assured of profitable disposal of their crop.

By the end of the Fourth Five Year Plan it was expected that India would be producing 40,000 tonnes of soyabean in 1 lakh hectares of land. The actual achievement, however, is only 57,000 hectares during a period of 13 years, i.e. about 4,385 acres per year.

The Central Government has also introduced an incentive scheme which offers subsidies to soyabean growers for purchasing pesticides and other inputs to the extent of one-fourth of the purchase price. This scheme is in accordance with the policy of the Government to encourage soyabean cultivation since it has been found to have a rich protein content and can be used as an additional source of edible oil.

During the Fifth Five Year Plan it was estimated that soyabean will be cultivated on 4 lakh hectares. But, as in the case of other oilseeds, this target also was not achieved. The production was a mere 80,000 tonnes.[23]

Use of Cottonseed Oil and other Oils in place of Groundnut

The Planning Commission had realized in the First Plan period the importance of cottonseed oil and since then had recommended its increased use. Also it had been encouraging the use of cottonseed oil in place of groundnut oil in manufacturing vanaspati. Even rebate in excise duty on the vanaspati manufacture out of cottonseed oil has been given. Nevertheless the industry has not taken to cottonseed oil.

Formerly the farmers believed that cottonseed had not other use excepting of a seed for growing cotton or as food for the cattle. At present however, the vanaspati industry is compulsarily using 30 per cent cottonseed oil.[24] Cottonseed oil has thus acquired a place of privilege in the production of vanaspati in India. Earlier it was not preferred because of its natural odour and deep colour. It was also costlier to refine. But with the shortage of groundnut oil and improvement in the refining techniques was not only permitted but on the other hand encouraged by the Government to be used for vanaspati manufacture. The all-India Cotton Crushers Association has played a very important role in encouraging use of cottonseed oil by the vanaspati industry. Whenever there is less intake of cottonseed in vanaspati manufacture the Association points it out and forces the Government to correct the situation. The Association has time and again stressed that the use of cottonseed oil should be on a batch-to-batch, day-to-day or even month to-month basis and not on the basis of a 'fixed' quantity during three to six months. The main consideration in introducing a minimum percentage of cottonseed oil in vanaspati manufacture was to ensure its use because it cannot be consumed directly.[25] It has also been stated that if properly encouraged and helped by the Government cottonseed oil can meet the entire oil shortage of the vanaspati industry at present met from imports. It will be explained by the following illustration. In a given year if the total production of cotton is 7.2 million lakh tonnes it will produce 2.4 million tonnes of cottonseed. If 0.2 million tonnes of cottonseed is set aside for use as seed for further production the total cottonseed available for crushing would be 2.2 million tonnes. If the entire seed is crushed 3.30 lakh tonnes[26] of cottonseed oil can be produced. If the total oil requirement for production of vanaspati is 5.3 lakh tonnes of groundnut (to the extent of 25 per cent) and sesame plus other oils (to the extent of 10 per cent) the total oil would be 1,85,500 tonnes. Total deficit of edible oil would thus be 5,30,000-185500=344500 tonnes. The deficit is broadly met by import of vegetable oils. If thc cottonseed oil is available to the extent of 3,30,000 tonnes as illustrated above, it can almost replace the entire imported oil and thus save the huge amount of foreign exchange spent for the import of this oil.

There are many 'ifs' and 'buts' in this proposition. First of all the entire cottonseed is not available. Mostly it is used as cattle feed. Very little is left for crushing. Also while crushing, the seed is not totally crushed. Sufficient quantity of oil is left in the seed. Another difficulty is that the vanaspati manufacturers still prefer groundnut oil to cottonseed oil. This is due to the fact that the groundnut oil is comparatively cheaper to refine. This is the reason why in 1976 one of the manufacturers of vanaspati used 72 per cent of groundnut oil and only 18 per cent of cottonseed oil though there was a statutory minimum limit of 25 per cent of groundnut oil and 30 per cent of cottonseed oil.

Other vegetable oils like mustard oil and linseed oil were tried for manufacture of vanaspati in the past. But because of the deep colour of the mustard oil and an unpleasant odour this oil was not found fit for use as a raw material for the manufacture of vanaspati.

Rice Bran Oil

Another potential oil which can augment the supply of edible oils in India is the oil extracted from rice bran. The economic possibility of this oil is great. A total quantity of 2 lakh tonnes of oil, at the rate of 14 per cent of the total bran available for extraction, could be made available. Value of this oil would be $60 million at the rate of 300 dollars per tonne.

Regarding the quality of oil extracted from rice bran, after refining, it may be mentioned that it has been accepted as one of the best edible oils. It has been proved chemically that because of a higher content of poly-unsaturated acids it is better than even the groundnut oil[27] and is as good as the sesame oil. Rice bran composition as given by the Rice Bran Commitee in 1961 is as under.[28]

Water	8.5—12.5
Protein	10.6—13.4
N. Free extract	38.7—44.0
Fat	10.00—22.0
Fibre	9.6—14.1
Ash	9.3—14.3
Penlosane	8.7—11.4
B. Vitamin (mg)	544

According to the Boso Oil and Fat Company Ltd., Japan, the oil contents of white rice bran of India with rice boiled and raw are 18.25 per cent and 12.15 per cent respectively. These are very substantial contents and can be used for augmenting the supply of oil for manufacture of vanaspati.

Properties of Rice Bran Oil

From the beginning the rice bran oil is sold to the soap industry for manufacture of laundry soap because the use of solvent extracted oil for edible purposes is banned in India. Rice bran oil can be refined and made fit for edible purposes as well but there is one snag. There is a loss of 30 per cent of the unrefined rice bran oil during the process of refining. It makes the refining very uneconomical. Recent researches in the oil technology have brought out one good quality in the rice bran oil which is not found even in groundnut oil and which justifies permission for lifting of the ban imposed by the Government of India for this oil being used as an edible oil. This is that rice bran oil contains less saturated fats as compared to groundnut oil which is regarded as one of the best edible oils in India.

Unsaturated fats, according to the experts, are of vital interest because of their effect in decreasing the level of cholesterol in human blood.[29] This oil has an advantage in preventing high blood pressure and alleviating hardening of the arteries.[30]

Japan has realized the importance of this great quality of rice bran oil and has become a pioneer in this industry by producing one-third of its total production of edible oil from rice bran.

Hydrogenated rice bran oil has the following other advantages.[31]

(i) It does not pick up flavours and odours of foods fried in it when it is used in cooking.

(ii) Food fried in the hydrogenated rice bran oil contains less fat than when fried in other oils.

(iii) The deoiled rice bran meal can be used not only as cattle feed but is also fit for human consumption when mixed with white wheat flour. This has been found out as a result of investigations by the Hawaii Agricultural Experiment Station in 1951[32].

(iv) The extracted rice bran can be used as fertilizer composition.

All said and done it is suggested that there should be no restriction whatsoever on the use of groundnut oil for vanaspati manufacture. Efforts should therefore be made to increase the yield of groundnuts in the country. This oil has clear advantages which outweigh the advantages of other oils. It is definite that if serious efforts are made it is not impossible to increase the yield of groundnuts in the country to the extent that the country may become self-sufficient in the groundnut oil requirements—for direct use as also for manufacture of vanaspati.

Suggestions and Steps taken for Improvement in Production of Oilseeds

Steps for quantitative improvement of production in the long run are :

(i) There should be specialized research centres for researches in oilseeds. This will result in both qualitative and quantitative improvement oilseed production in the country ;

(ii) The research instead of providing advice in a general way for all types of oilseeds and all crops of oilseeds should provide it for specific oil seeds and crops. This would be more useful and effective from the point of view of growers ;

(iii) Well-coordinated extension efforts should be made to

popularize the known practice for improvement of the quality of seeds. These should be supported by a seed multiplication programme. For example, 18 kgs. of groundnut seed can be multiplied into one lakh tonnes in three years' time.

(iv) There should be an intensive education programme for farmers in Gujarat, Punjab, U.P. and Rajasthan for increasing seed rates for groundnut crops. This can be done through means of mass media—radio and television. These can also be done through Block Level Workers.

(v) There should be development of techniques for agronomic yield for rising production of oilseeds without any additional acreage of oilseeds. This is very essential because the country does not have additional land for rising acreage under oilseed production.

(vi) It is further suggested that cultivation of sunflower should be encouraged. This can easily be done by growing it in the rice fallows and thus no additional land is required for this purpose.

(vii) There should be a buffer stock of 3-4 lakh tonnes of edible oils in the country. For this the Government should impose a levy on oilseeds of all types. This stock could be used during the period of rising prices due to bad crops. This will also encourage cultivators to grow at least that much quantity of oilseeds which they have to give to the Government as levy. The efforts of growers of oilseeds should not be confined to the extent of oilseeds required for levy but should encourage them to grow more and more oilseeds and sell them to private traders to get more money.

(viii) A national plan on oilseeds was announced[33] by the Government in 1976. Under this plan the aim was to augment the supply of edible oils in the country. The following steps were taken in this direction :

(i) A new directorate, known as Directorate of Oils

and Fats, has been set up to coordinate and implement the new oil policy of the Government.

(ii) The Government has already started announcing support prices for the oilseeds at national level to enable the growers to get remunerative prices for their products and also to take permanent measures in improving the yield of oilseeds.

(iii) The Government under the national plan takes into consideration the production prospects of various oilseeds, the anticipated requirements, the likely exportable surpluses of high-price oils against which low priced oils could be imported.

(iv) It has also been decided[34] to set up a national level corporation for edible oils. It will help in drawing up plans for augmenting the supply of vegetable oils and oilseeds.

These measures show that the Government has taken up this problem seriously. Frequent shortages of edible oils, fluctuation in the prices and resultant dissatisfaction of the general public is responsible for these steps to improve the over all supply of oilseeds and oil in the country.

No Miracle Oilseed in Sight

There is no miracle oilseed in sight which can revolutionize the oil supply in the country. It is only hard, well-directed mobilization of efforts on the part of the Government from the Village Level Worker to the agricultural scientist that can increase oilseed production.

Stability of Vanaspati

In the Western countries, because the climatic conditions are favourable and also owing to shorter distances and much better transport facilities there is no problem of shelf-life of fats and edible oils. But in India because of long distances, transport bottlenecks and extreme climatic conditions stability of fats and vegetable oil is a very big problem.

This is such an important problem that it has evoked discussions in the Estimates Committee of the Lok Sabha who asked[35] the Government as early as in 1961 to put down the dates on the packs themselves by which the contents of containers of vanaspati should be used. The Government also made provision in the Vegetable Oil Control Order of 1947 and empowered itself to check sale of contaminated vanaspati or stale vanaspati to consumers. According to an amendment in the Order every container should carry *inter alia* information about the month and year of production of the contents of the pack.[36] Printing of the expiry date on each container has not been agreed to by the Government on the plea that it is not being done either in the case of foodstuffs or on the packings of butter which is far less stable than vanaspati. This is not correct. People have a right to know whether the contents of a container are fit for consumption. It is, therefore, suggested that in addition to the information already printed on each of the vanaspati containers the date by which its contents should be consumed should also be indicated and for this, if necessary, suitable amendment may be made in the existing Order.

Another suggestion to improve the stability of vanaspati[37] is that the crude sesame oil instead of hydrogenated oil should be used in the making of vanaspati. It has been proved that the crude sesame oil is more stable than hydrogenated oil.

Low Oil Content in Indian Oilseeds

A deficiency in the oilseeds produced in India is that the recovery rate of oil is very low. This is also the reason for poor quality of oilseed in the country. According to the rates used by the Government to estimate oil production, Indian groundnut (shelled) and sesame can give 40 per cent recovery. Against this the relative recovery percentage of the world average for groundnut (shelled) and sesame are 43 and 47 respectively. This shows that in India not only the yield per acre is extremely low but the oilseeds are of poor quality as compared to those of other countries of the world.

The only answer to this is improved varieties of oilseeds. Sharp rise in per-acre yield of foodgrains in India is due to improvement in the quality of seeds as a result of extensive researches done in India and abroad. Such researches have not been undertaken in the case of groundnut. Although 'Asiriya

Nwitunde' a Tanganyika variety with many desirable qualities, has shown good response to irrigation and fertilizers when introduced at the Regional Centre, Hyderabad, through I.A.R.I., New Delhi, (the National Seed Corporation has been distributing this variety in different States) yet this has not shown desired results, viz. breakthrough in production of groundnuts as has been achieved in the case of foodgrains.

It is, therefore, suggested that the Government should order more researches for intensive cultivation of groundnuts of better quality so that the oil content could be increased. The following steps are suggested to augment production of vegetable oil in the country :

(i) Emphasis should be laid to increase yield per acre ;

(ii) Adoption of packages of practices and effective use of irrigation in potential areas ;

(iii) About 26.50 lakh hectares of additional areas should be brought under oilseed cultivation for maximizing production of groundnut and other oilseed.

Financial assistance which is being given to groups of oilseed should be continued ;

(a) Assistance to growers in the form of subsidy on plant protection chemicals and hand operated equipment should se continued,

(b) Grants should be given to the State Governments to cover full cost of additional staff appointed to look after the special scheme over and above the existing staff engaged in the Intensive Agricultural District Programmes for educating the growers covered by the schemes.

(iv) Emphasis should be laid on researches with the objective of stepping up the yield.

(v) Credit to farmers should be linked with production marketing ;

(vi) Large-scale demonstration plots should be laid. These should be shown to the oilseed grower so that he may go back and practise on his own fields.

(vii) Plant protection measures should be organised on a

campaign basis. Individual efforts cannot be of much help ;

(viii) Double cropping of groundnut, sesame and linseed over as large an area as possible under irrigation projects should be encouraged ;

(ix) Yields of oilseeds in the scarce rainfall areas should stabilized ;

(x) Cultivation of high-yielding varieties of groundnut in suitable areas should be extended ;

(xi) Minimum price of groundnut should be fixed so that the farmers may be assured of a reasonable price and may grow more groundnut. Although it is being done but the sales are not ensured.

High Prices of Edible Oils

Another problem faced by the vanaspati industry is the high price of edible oils especially the groundnut oil which sets the trends of prices of all edible oils. Rise in groundnut oil price has adversely affected growth of industry. According to the Planning Commission, "The demand (of vanaspati) has not expanded as rapidly as it would have if the price of oil had been lower."[38] This can very well give an idea of the importance of this problem. Hence the need of vanaspati industry is cheaper oil. Table 11.4[39] shows the index number of wholesale prices of groundnut and sesame oils—both used for production of vanaspati—for the period 1952-53 to 1968-69. The table shows continuous rise in the prices of groundnut.

TABLE 11.4

Index Number of Wholesale Prices of Groundnut and Sesame Oil for 1952-53 to 1968-69

(*Base year 1952-53=100*)

Year	Index no. of whole-sale prices	
	Groundnut Oil	Sesame Oil
1952-53	100	100
1956-57	103.8	121.8
1960-61	137.7	153.8
1964-65	168.3	172.8
1968-69	224.2	213.5

It will also be seen from Table 11.4 that the whole sale price index has recorded more than 100 per cent rise in the prices of both the groundnut and sesame oils during this period. The table also indicates that the prices of groundnut oil continuously rose upto 1961-62, and again from 1963-64. The prices of groundnut oil were highest in 1966-67 when the index number stood at 300.0 points.

The rising trend continued during the following two years, i.e. 1971-72 and 1972-73, when the average price of groundnut oil shot up to Rs. 6,885 per tonne.[40] During the following years the rising trend of prices did not stop. This is evident from Table 11.5.

TABLE 11.5

Wholesale Price Index[41] of Groundnut Oil during 1973-74 to 1977-78

Base year 1970-71

Year	Wholesale Price Index
1973-74	147.9
1974-75	172.4
1975-76	134.9
1976-77	142.8
1977-78	175.7

Thus the greatest problem for the industry is the rising cost of edible oil which the industry gets.

There is a close relationship between the prices of groundnut oil and those of vanaspati. High prices of groundnut oil have always resulted in a corresponding rise in the price of vanaspati. This fact can be verified from Table 11.6 which gives the prices of sesame, groundnut and vanaspati during April, 1976, to October, 1977.

The trend of groundnut prices during the decade 1961-1970 shows that they rose at the rate of 4.9 per cent in the first five-year period and at 10.6 per cent during the second five-year period. Also the output of groundnut declined at the rate of 2 per cent a year while the price increased by 9.7 per cent a

TABLE 11.6

Prices of Sesame, Groundnut and Vanaspati[42] during April, 1976, to October, 1977

Month/Year	Whole-sale prices of		
	Vanaspati (Rs. per 14.5 kg.)	Groundnut (Rs. per tonne)	Sesame (Rs. per tonne)
Apr. 1976	99.65	4500	5600
May 1976	99.10	4420	5600
June 1976	113.55	5600	6400
July 1976	119.55	5900	6400
Aug. 1976	123.90	7300	7400
Sept. 1976	123.90	6700	6600
Oct. 1976	123.90	5950	7200
Apr. 1977	147.00	9100	9300
May 1977	149.45	9500	9400
June 1977	151.45	9700	8700
July 1977	145.00	9100	8400
Aug. 1977	141.90	9100	8400
Sept. 1977	147.50	6900	6800
Oct. 1977	146.00	6400	7300

year. Again the prices of groundnut oil also rose, the main reason being an increase in the demand for it from both the consumer and the industry as a result of an increase in the population and the per capita income. The per capita consumption of vegetable oils which averaged 4.15 kg. a year in 1951-56, rose to 4.72 kg. in 1956-61, i.e. a rise of about 14 per cent; in 1961-62 it was placed at 5 kg. per head.

The demand for vegetable oil from both consumer and for production of vanaspati also rose. The consumption of vegetable oil increased from 12 per cent to about 18 per cent during the period 1950-51 to 1960-61.[43]

Another reason for rise in the groundnut oil price is the tendency of some State Governments to put restrictions on the inter-State movement of groundnut oil. The Government of Gujarat, for example, imposed a ban on 22 July, 1964, on the movement of groundnut oil outside the State to other parts of the country. Similar restrictions were imposed by the Gujarat and Tamilnadu Governments in 1976, also to check high prices of groundnut oil in their own states. But sometimes these restrictions and other acts of State Governments result in spurting the prices of groundnut oil as was found in 1974. The Gujarat Government imposed a levy on the groundnut oil to bring down its price in the market. Under an order the oil mills were obliged to surrender voluntarily 20 per cent of groundnut oil for making a buffer stock. Since there was no statutory obligation this did not prove effective and the prices of groundnut oil rose very high in the State. Gujarat State produces 25 per cent of the groundnut oil in the country and is the largest supplier of this oil to the vanaspati units all over the country. And such restrictions lead to sharp rise in prices of groundnut oil in the rest of the country.

Another cause of high price of edible oils in the country is the speculative trade in this commodity. In addition to the professional traders even the manufacturers of vanaspati indulge in forward sales. To prevent this, the Government of India has banned forward trading in edible oils especially groundnut, yet clandestinely the trade goes on and it results in the rising of prices of the groundnut oil in the country.

Besides the rising tendency in the oil prices another important problem which confronts the vanaspati industry is the fluctuations in the prices of oils. This makes the market quite unstable. And the Indian oil market is very unstable. A rise of 20 to 30 per cent and a fall of the same magnitude in the crop season is not uncommon in India. The urgent need of vanaspati industry, according to the Vanaspati Manufacturers' Association of India is 'stable prices of oil'.[44] There is no harm if the prices remain high but the manufacturers suffer most if the prices fluctuate. The manufacturers of vanaspati would surely be ready to cut prices in pursuit of extra production but lack of stability turns even a vanaspati dealer into a speculator making his living not through his earnings on the turnoner but through correct guessing of oil price variations. This has resulted in forward sales not only of oils but also of vanaspati by some traders. Even 'forward markets' in vanspati have sprung up in some places.

Table 11.7 shows the fluctuations in the prices of groundnut oil during 1962-70.

TABLE 11.7[45]

Highest and Lowest Prices of Groundnut Oil during 1962-1970

Year	Highest Price (Rs. per tonne)	Lowest Price (Rs. per tonne)
1962	2000	1665
1963	2000	1585
1964	3250	1765
1965	3700	1970
1966	5525	3375
1967	4750	2950
1968	4550	2320
1969	5350	2330
1970	5575	4200

It will be observed that fluctuations in groundnut oil prices have widened fourfold from an average of Rs. 500 up to 1963 to over Rs. 2,000 in 1968. Short-term fluctuations are still larger.

Agricultural Produce Markets Speculation

The markets of agricultural produce are speculative all over the world whether or not the speculative transactions are banned by the Government. Even in America where the Commodity Credit Corporation nurses large stocks under price support programmes fluctuations of the order of 20 per cent[46] in soyabean oil prices in a short period are not uncommon. So, in India where the oil demand and supply are in a precarious balance, even in times of bumper crops heavy fluctuations in oil prices are inevitable.

However, the Government tries to control these fluctuations by timely pumping in more or withholding supply of soyabean oil from the market complete eradication of this problem has not been possible so far.

It is, therefore, suggested that huge buffer stocks of

groundnut oil should be created. This would enable the Government to pump in more oil in the market whenever prices go up and make a purchase of oil whenever the prices go down. The Government should fix a support price for groundnut oil so that its price may not fall below that level.

But for long-rerm measures to prevent fluctuations in the prices of edible oil production of oilseeds in proportion to demand is the answer.

Packing

Shortages of Tin Plates : Vanaspati industry also suffer from shortage of tin plates. The result is that the manufacturers have to purchase these by paying more than the controlled price. Sometime the industry finds it even difficult to procure tin plates at a price well above the margin allowed to vanaspati manufacturers in the price formula.[47] This problem was emphasized by the VMA in the sittings of the Estimates Committee[48] as early as in 1960.

Besides resorting to packing in containers only 2 kg. and onwards another suggestion is that the Government should allot tin plate quota on the basis of actual requirements and not on the basis of total availability of tin plates in India. Vanaspati manufacturers, to ease the situtiion, have already introduced plastic containers on a very large scale. This has solved the problem of shortage of tin sheet for fabrication of tin containers somewhat. But there is a minus point, plastic containers are costlier. But the customer does not mind. These days both types of containers—tin and plastic—are in use for packing vanaspati in all sizes—1 kg., 2 kg, 4 kg. For packing 16.50 kg. of vanaspati only tin containers are used.

Further, in order to reduce the cost of tin plates, the Central Government, as was suggested at the Seminar on Packaging in 1967 in New Delhi,[49] should reduce the excise duty on tin plates.

Defective Credit Policy of Government

It has already been seen that whenever there is a rise in the prices of groundnut oil or vanaspati the Government, through the Reserve Bank of India, imposes restriction on the advances by the commercial banks to vanaspati manufacturers. This policy is unimaginative. It seems that the Reserve Bank of

India has only one answer to any rise in the prices of groundnut oil and that is to put a check on the credit advances. The R.B.I. seems to be following it blindly, without at all trying to analyse the causes of rise in the prices of groundnut oil. Credit curb is justified when there is a real shortage of groundnut oil in the country. But when the shortage is artificial these credit restrictions actually harm the traders instead of helping them.

For example, the RBI, on 25 January, 1971 imposed credit restriction in the wake of rising prices of groundnut oil. It was perhaps guided by the price statistics. Had it cared to analyse the causes of the rise in the groundnut oil prices it would have found that at the root of the price rise was the wide publicity given by the State Governments of Maharashtra and Gujarat and the Central Government about their intentions to build up buffer stocks of groundnut and groundnut oil. This resulted in credit squeeze and there was marked decline in the prices of groundnut oil—below the level prevailing in the corresponding period last year.[50]

These stereotype actions of the RBI do more harm to the industry and little good to the consumer. The prices of groundnut oil would not have gone up continuously because there was enough stock in the market. Another disadvantage of these restrictions is that at a time when there is need to increase production to meet a rising demand the restrictions on credit supply hinder progress.

Further, the purpose for which these restrictions are imposed have very little effect. For example, there was very little effect on the price fluctuations of the groundnut oil or vanaspati. It is well known that in oilseeds farmers have now developed a fairly strong holding capacity and they withhold stocks in the expectation of better prices. Further, large finances from other sources than the banks are available for trading in oilseeds and oils. Therefore the restrictions do not do any good to the trade and only harm the genuine manufacturers of vanaspati who do not indulge in speculative trading.

The Government should if it cannot do away with all the curbs in regard to credit limits to vanaspati manufacturers, swoop upon the professional speculators. Vanaspati manufacturers have to purchase and stock groundnut and groundnut oil in a low market so that they can increase the margin of profits in manufacturing vanaspati.

Transport

For the efficient working of an industrial establishment it is necessary that appropriate quantities of various raw materials are delivered in good time at the factory and also that the finished products are removed to the various centres of consumption. But these aspects involve adequate transport facilities.

Of the basic raw materials required for the manufacture of vanaspati, the major items are vegetable oil and coal. Tank wagons are the most economical way of transporting oil in bulk. Movement in oil drums and other small containers can also be arranged but it is inconvenient and involves loss of oil due to leakage (from 2 to 4 per cent) as well as cost and depreciation of containers. Further, the railways charge higher freight on these containers than for the tank wagons. For example, if the oils were to be moved in tank wagons instead of in drums there could be an overall saving of Rs. 70/- per tonne. This would come to four paise per kilogram in the cost of vanaspati.

Another problem of transport is faced in transporting imported oil from America to different parts of the country to feed the manufacturing units.[51] The Railways have to be persuaded every time to make special arrangements. During the crop season when the indigenous oil traffic is heavy the availability of tank wagons for transporting soyabean oil becomes extremely difficult. From the present situation of oil supply in the country it can be visualized that for the requirement of the vanaspati industry the transportation of imported oil will have to be continued for some time to come. In the absence of supply of adequate tank wagons it will be difficult to supply oil in time and avert losses in transit.

Unlike vegetable oil traffic the transport of coal does not require any special wagon. The difficulty faced by the industry in hauling the coal to the factories is due to the shortage of rolling stock. Possibility of transporting vegetable oil through pipelines should therefore be explored.

As regards transport of vanaspati from one place to another, at present the industry is moving most of its products by road despite higher freight incidence because of the difficulties in obtaining wagons in reasonable time. Small quantities of ordinary rolling stock are required. No special types of wagons are involved, and these too not many in number, yet there is difficulty.

More tank wagons should be allotted to vanaspati industry. Tank wagons should also be placed at the disposal of the State Trading Corporation as soon as it sends its requirements to the railways for transporting soyabean oil.

Problem of Power

The source of energy for turning the wheels of the industry has appreciable influence on the industrial development. Electricity and coal being the cheap source of power are used as fuel in the mills under study.

Consumption of electricity norm is 220 kwp per tonne. For manufacture of vanaspati it is given in Table 11.8.

TABLE 11.8

Requirements of Electricity for Vanaspati Manufacture[52]

Year	Production Capacity (000 tonnes)	Requirement of Electricity (kw/tonne)
1960-61	330	77
1965-66	550	121
1970-71	810	178
1975-76	1400	308

It will be seen from Table 11.8 that 308 kw of electricity was required for 14 lakh tonnes of vanaspati. (These estimates were drawn up by the Planning Commission.)

Similarly the consumption of coal for manufacture of vanaspati is also substantial. The industry consumed 725 lakh tonnes of coal in 1970-71. During the years 1975-76 the industry consumed 11 lakh tonnes of coal.[53]

Normally the production of one tonne of vanaspati requires 18 tonnes of coke.

As regards the requirement of non-cooking coke the consumption norm is that for production of one tonne of vanaspati 300 tonnes of non-cooking coke is required. On the basis of above norms the following Table gives consumption of non-cooking coke for manufacture of vanaspati:

Year	Requirement of coke (000 tonnes)	Requirement of non-cooking coke[54] (000 tonnes)			
		Steam	Stable	Middlings	Total
1970-71	13	220	—	—	220
1975-76	20	330	—	—	330

It will be seen that vanaspati industry has been using both sources of power.

However, coal is the principal fuel. It is required for boilers. Because of the short supply in the past, it has not kept pace with the demand. The prices of coal are soaring and supplies are erratic. The railways have adopted the system of priorities in allotting wagons to industries for coal movement. But to the great misfortune of this industry the entire vegetable oil industry including vanaspati which is an essential industry has not been given its proper place. Hence the industry has time and again been starving for coal. Now this industry has been included in the List of Industries which are treated on priority basis for allotment of wagons for coal.

To solve this problem some of the units have been using firewood, which is not a proper substitute. First, it is costlier than soft coke. Secondly, it is not sufficiently available.

Electricity

Another important source of energy which is used in the vanaspati industry is electric power. This is evident from the fact that during 1955 the industry consumed 95.85 kw of electricity. In 10 years time the consumption rose to 188.35 lakh kw, in 1965.[55] But the industry has to face some difficulties in this connection. In the first instance it takes at least two to three years in U.P. and one and a half years in Delhi area where the seven units have been located to get an electric connection. Further the rates of electricity in U.P. are higher than those in Delhi and other neighbouring States.

The difficulty with electric power especially in U.P. is that the voltage is very low. The load being high, there are frequent breakdowns.

It is suggested that the rates of electricity for this essential industry should be further reduced. In addition this industry should be included in the List of Industries which are given priorities for power connections. Further the power breakdowns should be completely eliminated. The industries in the whole country were hit very hard because of the inadequate supply of electricity on account of drought condition in 1979-80 in many parts of India. Vanaspati industry was however, exempted from the power cut because of the fact that any reduction in production of vanaspati would have hit the general consumer very hard.

Exports of Vanaspati

The Government of India, (Ministry of Commerce and Industry) introduced in October, 1959, an incentive scheme for stimulating exports of vanaspati. Under the scheme the losses which were suffered by the exporters of vanaspati due to lower prices of the product prevailing in foreign markets were to be offset by granting import licences for copra. The quantum of copra was to be such as to give the importers sufficient profits to compensate them for the losses suffered on account of export of vanaspati.

The Government allowed[56] import of copra to the extent of 109 per cent of the f.o.b. value of vanaspati exported. It also allowed exporters of vanaspati to import chemicals and equipment up to five per cent of the f.o.b. value of vanaspati exported.

The Estimates Committee also recommended[57] that the incentives under vanaspati export promotion schemes should be issued expeditiously.

The export of vegetable oil and vanaspati was banned in July, 1964. The exports afterwards were nominal to meet the commitment only. Since then the ban has not been lifted because the circumstances which had compelled the Government then to impose the ban are still prevailing. There is still shortage of vegetable oils in the country.[58]

Although there was shortage of vegetable oils for the manufacture of vanaspati in the country yet our trade missions

TABLE 11.9
Foreign Exchange Earned by Export by Vanaspati during 1951-52 to 1965-66

Year	Foreign Exchange Earned in lakhs
1951-52	75.3
1952-53	57.9
1953-54	21.1
1955-56	147.7
1956 (Apr.-Dec.)	175.0
1957 (Jan-Dec.)	164.0
1958	84.1
1959	52.7
1960 (Jan-March)	55.7
1960-61 (Apr.-Mar.)	13.6
1961-62	103.3
1962-63	55.8
1963-64	44.7
1964-65	62.1
1965-66	19.5

abroad had been asked for the first time to explore possibilities of exporting vanaspati. It was found that India could export vanaspati to West Asian and African countries.[59] These commodities are still in short supply in the country and as such no publicity in foreign countries for promotion of export to these countries has been undertaken. The position of vegetable oil supply has remained the same. The efforts on the part of the Government of India and unofficial organization like the VMA have not succeeded in bringing about a breakthrough in the edible oil supply position in the country. This is the only industry that can absorb the additional supply of oils and oilseeds. The installed capacity has recently increased manifold. But the annual consumption in the country is not likely to exceed 7 lakh tonnes in the next few years. The additional installed capacity should therefore be used for exports. Efforts should be made to publicize in foreign countries the values of our vanaspati so that within a couple of years when the industry utilizes its installed capacity and the production of oilseeds increase it could become a good foreign exchange earner. Vanaspati has potential markets in foreign lands. A little effort on the part of the Government and the industry could earn the much needed foreign exchange for the country.

Taxation

Another problem that the industry faces is high incidence of taxation which it is subjected to. Besides the corporate taxes which vanaspati manufacturing units—most of these are the joint stock companies—pay the products are subject to the following duties : (i) Central Excise Duty, (ii) Central Sales Tax, (iii) State Sales Tax, (iv) Octroi Duties.

Excise Duty : Excise duty on vanaspati was imposed as early as 1943 and still continues to be a feature of the tax pattern of the industry. It has, however, been periodically revised. Table 11.10 shows the rates of excise duty in different years.

TABLE 11.10

Rates of Excise Duty on Vanaspati, 1957-58 to 1975

Year	Rate of excise duty per tonne (in Rs.)
1957-58	112
1958-59	172
1961-62	200
1963-64	320 plus surcharge of 20% on excise duty amounting to Rs. 384 per tonne.
1965-66	200
1975	Re. 1 per kg.

The industry is an important industry from the point of view of revenue earning for the groundnut. During a year the industry pays Rs. 20 crores as excise duty to the national exchequer.

The need for reforming the present system of taxation and tax structure of vanaspati can hardly be emphasized. The main reform should be that the total number of taxes should be reduced. The Government should, in the first instance, impose uniform tax on the whole income of the companies. This will reduce the complexity and confusion prevailing between the various tax laws.

Another reform needed is in the administration of tax laws.

This should be simplified. It will result in reduction of tax litigation to the minimum. Indian entrepreneurs hesitate to invest because of protracted tax litigations. A review of the powers of the tax officers is now necessary. This will, on the one hand, lighten the burden of responsibility of those officials and, on the other safeguard the assessees from the possibility of harassment.

The taxation should be based on sound economic principles. The present policy of imposing taxes on the ground of pure expediency of collection of funds should be given up. On the other hand before imposition of taxes their long-term effects on the industry should be considered.

Sales Tax : The sales tax at the rates ranging between 5 and 6 per cent is charged for vanaspati. In 1957, a levy on inter-States sales tax at the rate of 1 per cent for sales between registered dealers at the prevailing rates in the exporting State was imposed. Prior to that there was uncertainty regarding the liability of the tax. It was then removed. But the drawback of tax evasion for which the inter-State sales tax was levied remained there.

Several times it has been suggested that sales-tax should be abolished and replaced by enhanced Central excise. This was suggested for the first time before the Taxation Enquiry Committee in 1953-54[60] but was not agreed to.

The manufacturers are in favour of the present arrangements regarding sales tax because (i) they do not have to maintain records, and it is easier for them to pay, and further there is no harassment from the State sales tax officials. It is because of the stiff opposition from the State Governments that the sales tax has not so far been abolished. The State Governments argue that (i) they would be deprived of the elastic source of revenue, (ii) they would have to depend upon the Centre for finances.

Vanaspati is a commodity which is consumed all over the country by the rich as well as by the poor. This therefore should be exempted from all types of sales tax. In addition there should not be any corresponding increase in the excise duty which is very heavy so that it may be available to the poor class of society at a cheaper rate. Because of the poor financial resources of the country it cannot be suggested that vanaspati should be totally exempted from all taxes—even excise duties—but the present rates of duties can certainly be reduced to the bare minimum. Ultimately, at the Chief Ministers' Conference held in the middle of 1980 a decision was taken. According to this the sales tax and octroi duties on vanaspati will be abolished and that they would be collected along with the excise duties from the manufacturers. Though this is a radical step and should have been taken long ago, yet it has not yet been implemented. The modalities are being prepared and it is hoped that soon the industry would be released of these cumbersome levies.

Further, vanaspati should be exempted from octroi duty also which is charged by several municipal boards. The following are the reasons why octroi duty on vanaspati should be abolished :

(i) The form in which these are levied offend all canons of taxation;
(ii) Their collection and system of refund put the person paying the tax to a great amount of inconvenience ;
(iii) It offers scope for fraud, evasion, underassessment, harassment, nepotism and extortion. It has been alleged that there is about 15 per cent leakage in collection ;
(iv) It allows great scope to the dodgers and evaders to indulge in malpratices;
(v) This tax is a burden on consumers especially who belong to the lower strata of society.

Low Profitability

The health of the industry is measured by two things, the goodwill it enjoys among the consumers and the efficiency with which it is run. The best yardstick of measuring efficiency is return on capital. Vanaspati does not offer adequate returns to the investors. According to a study of the RBI, gross profit as a percentage of employed capital was the lowest in vegetable industry (including vanaspati) during 1951-55. It was only 2.5 per cent[61] against the average of 9.2 per cent of all industries. The general notion about the industry is that it is a very profitable industry and that is why there is a rush to establish new

TABLE 11.11[62]

Gross Profit in Vanaspati Industry

Name of Industry	Gross Profit as % of Sales		Gross Profit as % of Total Capital employed		Gross Profit as % of Sales		Gross Profit as % of Total Capital employed	
	1959	1960	1959	1960	1965-66	1966-67	1965-66	1966-67
Tea	20.6	20.6	13.3	12.5	15.0	17.0	8.9	9.9
Edible vegetable oils and hydrogenated oils	4.3	3.1	10.3	7.5	3.2	3.8	9.6	12.8
Sugar	8.9	9.8	10.3	9.0	10.1	7.6	10.2	8.0
Cotton Textiles	6.3	9.2	8.3	11.8	4.5	6.0	6.7	5 3
Transport Equipment	8.1	8.7	9.6	10.7	11.1	10.5	10.9	9.1
Minerals	20.8	18.0	14.8	14.0	38.6	34.4	11.1	11.6
All cos.	10.0	10.2	9.8	10.1	9.9	9.5	9.6	9.3

units in the country. But the fact is that the net profit in the industry is the lowest among the organized industry in the country. This was evident fiom the information given by the RBI in its various bulletins. This has been compiled in Table 11.11.

TABLE 11.12[63]

Gross Profits as Percentage of Sales and Capital of 10 Companies with Predominant Interest in Vanaspati Industry 1963-64 to 1969-70

Year	Gross Profit	
	As % of Sales	As % of Capital
1963-64	3.2	13.4
1964-65	4.0	13.3
1965-66	3.9	15 0
1966-67	3.7	14.6
1967-68	1.7	7.2
1968-69	1.7	7.0
1969-70	1.5	6.9

The low profitability thesis of vanaspati industry is also supported by Table 11.12 which shows the gross profits as percentage of sales and capital of 10 leading companies having predominant interest in the vanaspati industry.

It can thus be seen that the profits have gone down both as percentage of sales and as percentage of capital since 1963-64. As regards reasons for the low profitability in the industry wherein huge capital has been invested, non-utilisation of installed capacity is the principal one.

Another compilation made by the NCAER shows that there is negative profitabily in the vanaspati industry. It has been shown in Table 11.13 which shows returns on the capital employed in vanaspati industry for the period 1966-1975.

It will be seen from Table 11.13 that except during 1970 throughout there was negative return of capital. During 1974 when the industry was in the deep crises the negative return rose to 50.8 per cent. Because of very low production there were huge losses to the industry.

The strange phenomenon noticed in the industry is that despite the low profitability the industry has a large number of

TABLE 11.13

Return on Capital[64] Employed in Vanaspati Industry for the Period 1966-1975

Year	Percentage of Return on Capital
1966	(–) 10.3
1967	(–) 10.4
1968	(–) 10.5
1969	(–) 1.5
1970	(–) 1.2
1971	(–) 8.2
1972	(–) 5.8
1973	(–) 12.1
1974	(–) 50.8
1975	(–) 17.6

investors. This is due to the fact that the investors get some return by selling the products at better margins of profit in the open market.

Trade Margin

In addition to the manufacturers the traders in vanaspati industry also expect a fair margin of profit so that vanaspati trade could be a profitable one. During the statutory control till June, 1952, trade margin allowed to wholesalers and retailers was Rs. 200 per tonne. This margin was continued when the informal price control was agreed upon in May, 1963. But the Government decided to reduce the total trade margin from Rs. 200 to Rs. 140 per tonne. So many agitations took place and representations were made when this decision was taken. Even the manufacturers represented to the Government that they would be adversely affected by the reduced trade margin but in vain. And it was after the Grain Dealers Federation of Bombay's petition to the Lok Sabha in 1967 that the Government increased the trade margin to Rs. 150 per tonne. They also fixed the margin of wholesalers and retailers at Rs. 70 and Rs. 80 per tonne respectively. The present rising prices of vanaspati have entailed a larger investment by the trading class. And the trade margins have been reduced. In order to save the consumer from a higher price of vanaspati, the Government should take over the wholesale trade of this essential commodity. It will ensure regular supply at cheaper rates to the consumers. Immediate steps should therefore be taken in this regard and the entire distribution of vanaspati should be done through cooperatives.

REFERENCES

1. *Lok Sabha Debates* 6th Series, Lok Sabha Starred Question No. 728 answered on 14.4.78.
2. *Lok Sabha Debates*, 6th Series, Vol. XXII, Pt. II, Lok Sabha Starred Question No. 172 answered on 22.3.1979.
3. *Lok Sabha Debates*, 6th Series, Vol. IX, Lok Sabha Starred Question No. 178 answered on 3.3.78.
4. Lok Sabha Debates, 6th Series, Vol. XXII, Pt II, Lok Sabha Starred Question No. 172 answered on 22.3.1979.
5. Commerce, Annual Number 1967, Bombay, p. 176
6. *India: A Reference Annual* 1979, Ministry of Information and Broadcasting, New Delhi, p. 20
7. *Oilseeds in India* (Brochure), Ministry of Food and Agriculture, New Delhi.
8. Vanaspati Manufacturers Association Note "Maximization of Capacity Utilisation and Productivity" presented at the meeting of the National Productivity Council held on 30-31 August, 1971, in New Delhi.
9. *VMA Annual Report* 1964, VMA, Bombay, 1965, p. 10.
10. *VMA* Reply to Questionnaire issued by the Tariff Commission, 1969.
11. *VMA Annual Report*, 1969, VMA, Bombay, pp. 16–17.
12. *Times of India Directory* 1979, Times of India Press, Bombay, pp. 60-61.
13. L. G. Kulkarni, *Groundnut in Indian Farming*, New Delhi, December, 1967.
14. L. G. Kulkarni, *Groundnut in Indian Farming*, December, 1967.
15. *Indian Agriculture in Brief*, Govt. of India, 1970, pp. 32 33.
16. S. S. Rajan, Genecist (Oilseeds), Division of Genetics, I.A.R.I., New Delhi, "Sesamum", *Indian Farming*, December, 1967.
17. *Lok Sabha Debates*, 6th Series, Vol. XXII, Lok Sabha Starred Question No. 172 answered on 2.2.1979.
18. G. S. Hattangadi, *The Vanaspati Industry*, Indian Central Oil Seeds Committee, 1958, p. 8.
19. ibid.
20. Maharajkumar Virendra Singh, "Soyabean Crop without a peer", *Commerce*, Annual Number 1965, p. 120.
21. *Lok Sabha Debates*, 4th Series, Lok Sabha Secretariat, 1969, Vol. 30, Unstarred Question No 1618 answered on 31 July, 1968.

22. ibid
23. *Times of India Directory*, 1979 Times of India, Bombay.
24. *Rajya Sabha Debates*, Rajya Sabha Secretariat, New Delhi, 1970, Part II, Vol. 69, 1969, Question No. 1730 asked on 29.8.1969.
25. "Cottonseed+Vanaspati" by K.S. Mahadevan, *Economic Times*, Bombay, dated 5.6.76.
26. Cottonseed and Vanaspati Industry, *Commerce Supplement*, 6 Sept. 1975, pp. 11-15.
27. *Industrial Development of Asia and Far East*, United Nations, 1966, Vol. IV, p. 283.
28. *Rice Bran Committee Report*, Government of India, 1961.
29. United Nations, Notification 24.
30. ibid., p. 284.
31. ibid.
32. ibid., p. 285.
33. *Lok Sabha Debates*, 6th Series, Vol. No. X, Lok Sabha Unstarred Question No. 682 asked on 24.2.78.
34. *Lok Sabha Debates*, 6th Series, Vol. X, Lok Sabha Unstarred Question No. 738 asked on 24.2.78.
35. Estimates Committee (2nd Lok Sabha), Lok Sabha Secretariat, New Delhi, 1961, *127th Report 1960-61*, p. 31, para 63.
36. Ministry of Food and Agriculture (Deptt. of Food), O.M.No. 9-1/6-s. Adm. dated 17 Oct, 1961, addressed to Lok Sabha Secretariat.
37. Hattangadi, n, 18. p. 68.
37. *Planning Commission, Programme of Industrial Growth 1951-56*, Planning Commission, New Delhi.
39. (i) *Rajya Sabha Debates*, Vol. 59 (1967), Unstarred Question No. 119, asked on 30.3.1967, Rajya Sabha Secretariat, New Delhi.
(ii) *Rajya Sabha Debates* Vol. 69 (1969), Unstarred Question No. 1730 asked on 29.8.1969, Rajya Sabha Secretariat, New Delhi.
40. Compiled from the figures given in reply to Lok Sabha Unstarred Question No. 443 answered on 25.3.74, *Lok Sabha Debates*, Vol. 37. Lok Sabha Unstarred Question No. 10192, *Lok Sabha Debates*, 6th Series, Vol. XV.
42. *Rajya Sabha Debates*, Vol. No. C III No. 10, Rajya Sabha Unstarred Question No. 553 answered on 29. 1.77.
43. *Export of Vegetable Oil & Oilseed*, NCAER, Aug. 1965. Table p. 19.
44. VMA *Annual Report 1962*, VMA, Bombay.
45. VMA *Annual Reports 1962-1970*.
46. VMA Reply to Questionnaires issued by the Tariff Commission, 1969.
47. *Commerce*, 7 May, 1968, p. 806.
48. *Estimates Committee (1960-61) Report*. (2nd Lok Sabha), Lok Sabha Secretariat, New Delhi, 1968, No. 127, 1960, p. 22.
49. *Report on the Seminar on Cost Reduction in Packaging* organized in 1967, Indian Institute of Packaging p. 49.
50. *Commerce*, 29 May, 1971, p, 993.

51. *Lok Sabha Debates*, 4th Series, Vol, 7, Unstarred Question No. 1317 asked on 27.7.1967
52. *Notes on Perspective Development, India*, 1960-61 to 1975, Planning Commission, pp. 76-77.
53. *Notes on Perspective of Development, India, 1960-61 to 1975*, Planning Commission, (Table c-1) pp. 68-69
54. ibid.
55. *A Report on the Census of Indian Manufactures and Survey of Industries*, Central Statistical Organisation, Deptt. of Statistics, Calcutta.
56. Estimates Committee (1960-61), *Second Lok Sabha Report No.* 127 1960, p. 33.
57. ibid, p. 960.
58. *Rajya Sabha Debates*, Part 2, Vol 58, Nos. 13-25, Unstarred Question No. 696 asked on 5.12.1966.
59. *Lok Sabha Debates*, 4th Series, Vol. XVI, Unstarred Question No. 7028 asked on 11.4.1968.
60. *Economic Times*, Bombay, 24 June, 1971.
61. *R.B.I. Bulletin*, May, 1951.
62. (i) *R. B. I. Bulletin*, December, 1960.
    (ii) *Eastern Economist*, Annual Number, p. 13,39.
63. VMA Reply to Question No 1 of the Questionnaire issued by the Tariff Commission of India.
64. Price Control & Vanaspati Industry, NCAER, New Delhi, p. 72.

Index

Accessibility to Markets, 30ff
Agricultural Produce Markets Speculation, 137ff
All-India Cotton Crushers' Association, 125
American law (food industry), 101
Amritsar Oil Works (Amritsar), 77
Andhra Pradesh (oil seeds), 120
Asiriya Nwitunde' (a Tanganyika Variety), 132

Bandovin test (colouring of vanaspati), 98
Banking facilities, 32ff
Bleaching Earth (to decolorize the vegetable oil), 53
Bombay, 27, 32, 102
Bose Oil and Fat Company Ltd. Japan, 127
Butterine (margarine), 18

Calcutta, 32, 102
Capital Investment in Vanaspati Industry, (1953-77), 75t
Cheap Motive Power, 31ff
Chemical Industry, 18
Colouring agent, qualities of, 96; material, choice for, 97
Cooling (vanaspati manufacture, stage), 83ff
Cost Structure, 81ff
Cotton Seed Oil *see* Sesame Oil, 27, 38, 48;development of, 48ff; production of, 50t; quantity of (used in manufacture of vanaspati), 51t; use of, 125ff; Milling in Different States, Capacity of, 49t
Council of Industrial and Scientific Research, 92
Crude Sesame Oil, 131
Cultivation Cost, Reduction in, 118ff

'Dalda ghee' *see* synthetic fat
Decontrol, Effect of, 109ff
Delhi, 32, 102
Denmark, 20
Depreciation on Plant and Machinery and Building, 84ff
Desai, Morarji (Finance Minister), 103
Development and Regulation Act, 1951, 101
Distribution Rebate and Commission, 86

'Edible ghee', 93
Edible Oils, High Prices of, 133ff; shortage of, 113ff; vegetable oils, 37
Electric Power, Generation of (Major Power Projects), 32t
Electricity, Requirements of (for vanaspati manufacture), 141t
Essential Commodities Act, 1948, 101
Essential Supplies (temporary powers) Act, 1946, 102
Excise Duty on Vanaspati (1957-58 to 1975), Rates of, 145t
External Economies, 35
Extraction of oil, methods of, 48

Filter and Nickel catalyst (chemical used in production of vanaspati), 53

Financing Vanaspati manufacturers, source of, 77
Five Year Plan Periods, 23-24, 50, 52, 116, 124; consumption, 89; development, 39ff; production and consumption, 59ff
Food Corporation of India, 124
Foreign exchange earned by export of vanaspati, 144
Future Oil Requirements, Projection of, 43ff

Ganesh Flour Mill Co. Ltd., (Lyallpur), 22, 77
Ghaziabad, 32
Ghee, adulteration of, 98
Ghee Adulteration Committee, 95, 97; consuming states, 90
Government Hydrogenatic Factory (Kozhikode, Kerala), 77
'Green Revolution', 90
Gross Profit in Vanaspati Industry, 148-49t
Groundnut, Production of, 38t, 46t
Groundnut and Sesame, Per-acre Yield of, 115t; and Sesame Oil, Index Number of Wholesale Prices, 133t
Groundnut Oil, 27, 38; Prices of, 1962-70, 137t; production of, 46; Wholesale Price Index of, 134t
Gujarat, 27, 117, 120, 129, 136

Hindustan Lever Ltd. (Bombay), 22; Steel Limited, 85
Hindustan Vanaspati Manufacturing Company Ltd., 22
Hippolyte Mege Mouries (French-chemist), 18
Holland, 20, 95
Hydrogen Generation (stage of manufacture of Vanaspati), 82ff
Hydrogenated oil *see* Synthetic fats
Hydrogenated rice branoil, advantages, 128; vegetable oils, 19
Hydrogenation, 21; process of, 20, 83

Indian Agricultural Regional Centre, Hyderabad, 120
Indian Agriculture Research Institute, Delhi, 121, 124
Indian Council of Medical Research, 93
Indian National Food Congress, 52; Vanaspati Industry, 23
Indian Vegetable Product Limited Bombay, 21
Indian, Veterinary Research Institute Izatnagar, 92
Industrial Finance Corporation, 33; Peace, 35ff
Intensive Agricultural District Programme, 132

Kanpur, 32
Karmarker, D.P., (Health Minister), 93

Labour Vanaspati Industry, view of, 78
Licensing for Vanaspati, 24
Low Oil Content in Indian Oilseeds, 131ff
Low Profitability, 147ff

Madhya Pradesh, 48
Madras, 27, 32, 102
Maharashtra, 27, 29, 117
Mahatma Gandhi, 23
Major Oil Seeds, Year Wise Yield of, 41t
Manpower, availability of (development of industry), 30
Margarine, 19, 56, 88, 91
Margarine, Land and other Prepared Fats, Production of, 58t; World Production of, 57t
Margarine and Margarine—like fats, Per Capita Consumption, 20t; Production, Policies on, 100ff
Mysore, 27, 117, 120

Napoleon III (Emperor of France), 19

National plan on oil seeds, 1976, 129; seed corporation, 121, 132
Nutrition and vanaspati, 91ff

Octroi duty on vanaspati, reasons, 147
Oils, Pattern of use of, 45t; qualities of (using in production of Vanaspati), 37-38
Oil seeds, diseases of, 118; Production of, 42ff, 128; storage of, 122
Oil Seeds Growers, Fair Prices to, 121ff; Required for use in Vanaspati Manufacture, 44ff
Olao (oil discharged), 19
Oleomargarine Act, 1886, 91, 100

Packing, 138; *Defective Credit Policy of Government*, 138ff; *Shortages of Tin Plates*, 138; *Transport*, 140
Pagelar, Glenn L. (President of the Soyabean Council of America), 51
Pal, A.K., 92
Post-war Reconstruction Committee, 23
Power, Problems of, 141
Price Control, Effect of, 106ff; Pattern of (on Vanaspati), 103ff; Zonal Pattern of, 66ff
Production and Area Under Oil Seeds, Targets of, 42t
Punjab, 117, 129

Rajasthan, 117, 129
Rajendra Prasad (Food Minister), 92
Raw materials (for Vanaspati), 18, 37
Raw material—Oriented industry, 28, 31
Ray, A.K., 92
Recruitment, System of (Vanaspati Industry), 79ff
Regional Centre, Hyderabad, 120
Return on Capital Employed in Vanaspati Industry, 1966, 75
Rice Bran Committee, 1961, 126; Oil, 126ff
Rourkela Steel Plant, 85

Salaries and wages (members of the staff of the factory), 84
Sesame, Groundnut and Vanaspati, Prices of (April 1976 to October 1977), 135t
Sesame Oil, 27, 38, 47, 96, 102; Production of, 47ff
Soap Stock, 27
Soyabean, Promotion of Production of, 123ff
Soyabean Oil, 51ff, 107; Strategy for (in Fourth Plan Period), 52ff
Spectacular Progress during Plan Holiday (1966-67 to 1968-69), 63
State Trading Corporation, 105, 110, 123
Statewise Groundnut Irrigated Area, 121t
Sugar Industry, 113
Synthetic fat, 18, 21, 100

Tamil Nadu (vanaspati producing units), 27, 120
Tariff Commission, 105
Tata Oil Mills Company Limited, 22
Taxation, 145ff
Tin Containers, Number of (1955-65), 54t; Plates (raw material), 53ff
Trade Margin, 150ff
Trade Union movement in vanaspati Industry, 79
Transport Facilities (development of industries), 29ff

United States of America, 51, 91-92, 101, 106
Units of Vanaspati, Regional Distribution of, 28t
Urban areas, 27, 30
Uttar Pradesh, 32, 129

Vanaspati, 21ff, 56ff; colouring of (recommendations), 98; Consumption, Production and Installed capacity of (during First Plan) 60t; (during Second Plan), 61t, (during Third Plan), 63t; cost of

Production of, 81; Estimate of Consumption of (1969-74), 64t; Export of (1951-52 to 1955-56), 60t, 143; Percentage Distribution of (zonal distribution), 91t; Production of, 57, 59t; 65t; Production and Installed capacity of, 64t; Production Units of, 68t; Purpose of Consumption of, 66t; Regional Pattern of Consumption of, 70t, 90t; Regional Pattern of Production of (1962-70), 69t; Sale of (1935-46), 88t; Stability of, 130ff; Zonal Pattern of Production of (1966-76), 71t; Zonal Pattern of Production and Consumption of, 72t

Vanaspati Consumption, effects of, 92

Vanaspati factories, 21, 34; Ghee (Definition), 21; Industry, 15, 27, 75, 113, 125; Different Categories of Workers in, 78t; Working and Fixed Capital Investment, 76t

Vanaspati Manufacturers Association of India, 22, 24, 50, 89, 103, 117, 136

Vanaspati Manufacturing Units, 145

Vanaspati—Producing Units, 27-28

Vegetabte oils 37, 43ff; Import of, 114t; Processing of, 82-84

Vegetable oil control order, 1947, 131; Product Control Order, 102

Western Countries, 92, 95

Work and Loss of man-hours (1967-68) in West Bengal, 35t